I WANT TO BUY YOUR PRODUCT...

HAVE YOU SENT ME A LETTER YET?

How to create powerful sales letters, advertisements, flyers, brochures, web pages and newsletters that persuade hundreds, or even thousands, of customers and clients to buy from **you!**

Carol A E Bentley

Sallyann

with best wishes

Carol B

Published by Sarceaux Publications
London, England
ISBN 0 9549206 0 0
© Cover Design by Castle Direct

Catalogue Data

Bentley, Carol A. E.
    I Want to Buy Your Product... Have You Sent Me a Letter Yet?

    1. Copywriting 2. Marketing 3. Direct Response Marketing
    4. Business Development

Carol Bentley, one of the highest paid copywriters in the world, reveals in this
book the powerful, but little used techniques that double, triple or even
quadruple the number of customers coming to your business, often in just
weeks.

If you would like to talk to Carol's office about having her work on your
current or next sales project call freephone 0800 015 5515 or send an email to
info@carolbentley.com or return the enquiry slip on page 151.

USE THESE POWERFUL TECHNIQUES TO BOOST SALES, GAIN NEW CUSTOMERS AND ENJOY A DISTINCT ADVANTAGE OVER YOUR COMPETITORS!

"Having used direct response marketing techniques since the year 2000, the 'masterful' methodology described in this book has gone on to enhance sales by a further £99,500 from just one five page letter mailed to 3218 prospects. It goes on to prove that long letters do sell providing they are interesting and provide a compelling offer - all covered in page 65, chapter 9. I would recommend this book all day long. It is fun, interesting and EXTREMELY profitable!"

Anthony van Dort
Managing Director
Liberty Leisure

"Outstanding! It shows you an easy way to transform mediocre letters to explosive letters - the kind that get noticed, get read, get sales!"

Dr. Joe Vitale, author of way too many books to list here,
including "The Attractor Factor" www.mrfire.com

"Carol has obviously studied copywriting with great intensity, utter dedication and with total passion. To be as good as she is - she must have learned from all the experts, read all the books, gone to the best seminars, and listened to the tapes - everything.

So have I...and thanks to all the "gurus" I have become a top notch copywriter - and thankfully making lots of money. But here's the thing - I have spent 20 years and close on to £35,000 to learn the skills - and virtually ALL of them are in Carol's book which you can buy for under 15 quid.

If only Carol had written her book years ago...not only would I have found fame and fortune...I would have saved £34,985.05! So not only can YOU become a world class copywriter...you can do it with a few hours of study...and for a pittance.

If ever you needed the luckiest break you'll ever find...you've found it!"

Steve King
Copywriter,
Devon, England, UK

"I found the book very enjoyable and interesting."

Stephen Berger
Harry Berger Dry Cleaners

"Your advice is much more broadly applicable than just letters, and the workshops/ 'take-aways' are REALLY good."

Steve Bower
Seven Communications Ltd

"We got a 262% increase in response to our mailing, resulting in £24,101 worth of bookings, which included 30 new companies attending our courses. This is an impressive result for us."

David d'Orton-Gibson
Managing Director
TFP Online Ltd

"Well having purchased your book at the event, we swiftly put some of your ideas into practice. Our previous mailing letter went in the bin, and a refreshed version was generated. It is fair to say that the response level we now get has vastly increased. Not only in terms of immediate response, but also from those who have obviously retained our information and called some months later. We look back at our previous attempt and cringe."

Andy Littlecott
Buckfield Environmental, Buckfield Group

"I know Carol's writing methods work because I have tried several and they have had a dramatic impact on improved response rates. One letter produced a 19% response within 48 hours. Carol's book may change your life.

Brian James
Chairman
The Brian James Group

"I have quickly grown to admire Carol's skill as a business copywriter. She is ONE copywriter I would be happy to suggest many, many business owners and professionals employ to write advertising, sales letter, brochure and web site copy for their products, services or treatments."

Paul Gorman
Gorman Consulting

"I was getting 29 clicks per day. Then I changed my ad (on Google). This is getting close to 100 clicks per day! More than triple the number of people to my site! Just did what you said - provided a headline that would interrupt a person from their day and tried to hit their emotions – and the results are just amazing!"

Sadhiv Mahandru,
www.NaturalElements.co.uk

"When I read the incredible insights in Carol's book ... I was, to be honest, quite shocked by what I learnt. My letters were actually NOT based on the correct principles of explaining the Benefits of the Services I provide my clients.

I wasn't a long way off - but Carol's book really uncovered what I should be saying. I am now rewriting all of my existing materials.... and I know the increased response will make that exercise worthwhile."

Edward Rivis
Managing Director
Sumatrix Ltd

"A refreshing read that remains engaging to the last page. I was impressed with the multitude of examples and the regular use of questions and targets throughout, all gearing you to remain focused. Altogether a highly informative book aimed at all learning styles and all levels of sales marketing whether you're a novice starting out on your first mail shot or you just need some tips on refining your style."

Deonne Connelly
BLH High-Care

"At first I thought your book would be a daunting read but I was wrong! I found your book to be very informative and shows me that I CAN and SHOULD write my own copy for my business.

Your style of writing is easy going, informative and uncomplicated which gives me more confidence as I have the understanding to write my own copy now, perhaps a copywriting course as a next step?"

Azi Azhakesan

"It is so clear and methodical. I've learnt the theory (of copywriting) from others, but now your book puts it into a logical and 'followable' order, with lots of practical added tips and details. I shall be referring to it often. With the easily identifiable sections, practical examples and step-by-step workshops to guide the reader through each phase, it is a very useful desktop handbook to 'perfect' my marketing letters."

Janet Browne,
Managing Director
BLH High-Care

"I have just finished reading your book and I think it is excellent I am sure I will refer to it often. Definitely essential for every business's book shelf and it has the best advice on web sites I've ever seen."

Jeannie Monaghan
The Buxton Dental Practice

Dedicated to my loving husband,
Mark, who has never wavered in his
belief in me and who has supported
me in all my endeavours.

Contents:

Chapter 1

Why Bother to Write to Your Prospects?

There are hundreds, if not thousands, of people out there who would love to buy your product or service - if they only knew what it could do for them. If they understood how it would make their life better, appreciated the *real* result and benefit they would experience if they bought from you.

But they don't know. Why? Because you haven't reached them yet.

It doesn't matter how good your product or service is, how fantastic it makes people feel, how it finally resolves a major problem for them, if <u>you</u> do not tell <u>they never know</u> - and they never purchase from you.

Marketing is the lifeblood of your business. If you don't market your business; your products or services - you are denying all those people the opportunity to improve their life, in whatever way it could be enhanced, as a result of using what you offer.

But, perhaps you *are* doing the marketing, advertising and giving out brochures, yet you are still not getting the business you want. What can you do?

'When you decide you want more business, more sales, more customers or clients - BETTER results in fact - how do you get them?'

This is the question I'm asked time and time again. People want to know "How _can_ I convince someone what I offer is vitally important to them?"

The answer?

Simple - **tell him.** Use every means you possibly can to get your message in front of your target audience.

Find the people who have expressed an interest in your product or service. People who've already bought something similar are often attracted to what you offer. Write to them. **Send a letter!**

Explain to your prospective customer <u>exactly what she can expect to get</u> when she buys from you. How you can improve her life, take away a pain, solve a problem – whatever result you can provide – that's what you emphasise.

People, whether for business or for themselves, buy with high expectations. There are others who disbelieve anything they purchase ever has a profound effect for them.

Disappointment after buying is known as 'Buyer's Remorse'. It's your job to make sure your customer appreciates what she can expect from your product or service so she gets exactly what you are promising and is not, therefore, disappointed after buying.

Of course you need the skill to communicate your message in writing. In fact, it is very easy to give people the story behind your product or service and tell them what you can do for them, ***when you are face-to-face***. But writing it down; in letters, brochures, and all the other myriad of marketing media used to get people to buy, is sometimes a challenge.

How This Book Helps You to Increase Your Sales

You *can* write about *your* service or product. *You* are the expert. You have the passion and experience. Given half the chance, I'm sure you can 'wax lyrical' about your product or service.

Chances are it is only when you sit down to write the 'words just don't come'. And that's where this book helps you.

It introduces you to the concepts behind 'writing to sell'. It advises you on how to write your sales letters. And you'll discover this method applies equally to sales brochures, adverts, newsletters, web pages - in fact anything you produce in print to market your business.

I've also included the checklists *I* use:

- A checklist to help you prepare so you are writing to the best of your ability.

- A checklist that helps you to make sure you have included all the techniques (you're about to discover) in your sales letter, and...

- A checklist to create the most responsive order form you possibly can.

Read tips on how to get started and how to overcome writer's block.

Discover why the way you write your sales letter is critically linked to your success in business.

Appreciate why your opening gambit is crucial to getting your letter read and how you can build in a 'second chance' to draw your reader in.

In fact, you learn how to make your sales letter so

fascinating *and relevant* your prospect won't be able to put it down. More importantly, *your* writing compels them to take immediate action - the action *you* want them to take.

My first piece of advice is to make this book <u>work for you</u>. Make sure you pick up on the important tips <u>as they are revealed</u>. Use a highlighter to mark passages that are particularly significant for you. Make notes in the margin, circle important advice.

Doing this does not invalidate my guarantee.

Why do I make this suggestion?

When you look back through the book you can pick up the important gems again. You don't have to re-read all of the text just to pull out the particular point, which is vital to you and the letter you are writing at that moment.

One of the challenges we have as business people is we are always 'busy' and sometimes our 'busy-ness' prevents us following through when we discover new ideas which are beneficial to us or our business.

So, the other strong advice I'm giving you, is to take action at the end of each chapter, and...

Create Your Own Reference Points

If you absorb information by *reading*, transfer the points you have highlighted to your own 'notebook', so you can review it at any time.

If you learn best by *doing* - as so many people do - then take time to complete the workshop activities. This develops and builds your skills.

If you recall things you are *told* more easily, then

you probably get better results by recording the main points you've picked up and listening to them frequently, so you are imbued with the principles.

So, let's get started with writing your successful sales letters...

Chapter 2

Who are You Writing to and Why?

Before you even put pen to paper ask yourself some questions. Be very clear about the answers you give yourself.

1. Who are you writing to?

Have a very clear picture in your mind of the person you are writing to. Is it a man or a woman? What age is he/she? What are her interests? What is her lifestyle? What incentive does she need to buy? What problem does she have that needs solving? What makes her feel good? What makes her happy or sad? What is her business about? What is she looking for to help her in her personal or business life?

If you don't know what the person you are writing to is like and what 'turns her on' how can you possibly write a letter to her she understands, that excites her <u>and</u> motivates her to take action on?

Notice I'm talking about the '*person*' you are planning to write to. You must construct your letter as if you are writing to an individual. Your reader must feel as if you are <u>only</u> writing to her, even if you are writing to someone at a company.

If your letter reads as if you are sending it to a

large audience, the impact is lost because the recipient knows she is just one of a whole bunch of people you are trying to sell to.

Answer these questions about your recipient before you start any writing project:

- Is your reader male / female?
- What age group?
- What educational background?
- Is he/she employed, retired or unemployed?
- If employed, in what job position?
- What is he/she earning?
- What disposable income is available?
- What is his/her lifestyle?
- What interests does he/she have?
- What health and fitness levels?
- Is he/she married, living with a partner, divorced or single?
- Does he/she have children? If so, what age group?

In business:
- Is he/she the decision maker?
- Can he/she influence the decision maker?
- Is he/she responsible for a budget?
- What problem does he/she have that you can resolve?

You will not have a specific answer for some of these, or the question may not be directly relevant to what you are offering. But do consider these questions and at least make an informed guess as to what the answers might be. It helps you to compose the letter from your reader's point of view. It helps you to develop convincing reasons for buying your product or service right now.

Once you have a clear idea of your reader, give him/her a name and identity in your mind. Now write to that person, as if he/she were a close friend. Your letter must be friendly and informative - not an obvious 'selling letter' – one she is interested in reading and responding to.

2. Do you already know this person?

Is the person you are writing to an existing customer or client? Has he bought from you previously and, perhaps, allowed his relationship with you to lapse?

Is it someone who is not yet aware of what you offer and, maybe, hasn't even heard of you before? Or perhaps he currently buys from a competitor and you want to encourage him to change.

The relationship you have with the person you are writing to has a direct affect on your writing style and content.

The letter you write to an existing customer is very different to one you write to a lapsed buyer.

Providing, of course, your existing customer is happy with what you are already supplying, he does not need to be convinced of what you provide and the results he receives. All you need to do is encourage him to place a higher order value and purchase more frequently.

When you write to a past customer you remind him about the good results he has already experienced in the past and you encourage him to buy again.

Your letter to a new prospect, who has no experience or knowledge of you, is informative about the benefits you offer. But, be careful, when it is your first letter to him you must resist the temptation to launch into a self-aggrandising missive he has no interest in, and worse, may disbelieve.

3. Why are you writing?

What is the outcome you want? What action do you want your reader to take? Are you looking for a sale? A request for information? Do you want him to call you, visit your premises, email you or complete and send a form back to you?

Are you looking for an appointment or do you just want to confirm you have the contact details correct, ready for future mailings?

Whatever result you want you must keep this in mind whilst composing your letter. In your letter, tell him clearly <u>how to take the action you want</u>.

4. What is your offer?

Does your offer match the profile of your reader? Is she interested in the results and benefits you are offering?

Are you **sure**?

How do **you** know?

What research have you done to be confident your product or service supplies a result your reader is delighted with?

All this is part of targeting your audience - making sure you have the highest possibility of finding the people who *take the action* you are suggesting in your letter.

5. What is your guarantee?

If you are writing with the intention of getting a sale offer some sort of guarantee. Reassure your reader there will be no regrets after placing an order with you. Give every confidence taking up your offer is the best opportunity and the right decision for him/her.

Experience has shown the longer the guarantee is, the less likely you are to have returns. This is obviously assuming your product or service is as good as you claim.

When you offer a 30-day return policy, your buyer is more conscious of the timescale and it is at the front of his/her mind. If there is the slightest doubt about the result, he/she is more inclined to take up the guarantee.

With a 12 month guarantee there isn't the same sense of urgency. If the purchaser is a little unsure he/she will probably 'wait and see how it goes' before making a final decision. The longer timescale gives more time to get used to the product or service and appreciate the results gained. Consequently there are fewer returns or cancellations.

Workshop: Define Your Audience and Offer:

Thinking about your next writing project...

1. Write a description of your prospective reader.

2. Use the questions in this chapter to picture how he/she looks, talks and what interests him/her.

3. Decide what would appeal to your reader about the offer you are making.

4. Consider what outcome you want from your letter.

5. What guarantee can you give your prospect so he/she has the confidence to buy (if you are looking for a sale)?

Chapter 3

Know What Your Customer is Worth

All businesses want new customers. But sometimes concentrating on acquiring new customers can mean the potential from existing customers is ignored.

It is a lot easier to get a satisfied customer or client to buy again or buy more from you than to get new business. It is also a lot less expensive. Often, just writing to your existing customers regularly is all it takes.

Unless your business can only ever make a *single sale* to a new customer - and there are very few who are in that difficult situation - the majority of the value in your customer is in the sales *after* the initial purchase.

Most business owners and managers know this. I'm sure you do. However, not many people really appreciate the life time value of their customers.

When you know the **true** life time value then you know how much you can afford to spend on marketing or special offers in order to attract the first purchase.

Your Highest Profit Usually Comes from Subsequent Sales...

Let me give you an example:

Suppose you sold an electronic gadget, which normally retails at £50. It costs you £20 to buy. When someone purchases the gadget you make a gross profit (GP) of £30.

Having purchased that one item you keep the customer informed of similar products. They buy another piece of equipment at £150, which costs you £80 to buy. Giving you a GP of £70.

So far you've made £110. Now, let's say he purchases an item for £230, which costs you £110 to buy in. That's another £120 to add to your GP from that one customer.

Suppose he only buys one more item from you at £320, which costs you £180 at source: your overall GP is now £370.

Now you have this information you can make an educated decision on how you can encourage the first purchase. In fact you could afford to offer your first electronic gadget at a ridiculously low price, i.e. cost or even below, knowing that your marketing method - regular, informative contact - encourages more sales on which you can make your profit.

So, if you offer your first gadget at £21 instead of £50 as a 'special offer' you have a higher response of people purchasing than you if you tried to retain your profit margin on the first sale.

Don't forget, it's the follow-up nurturing that creates your *full* life time value.

Would you rather have 20 sales at £21 with the likelihood of further purchases creating a good gross profit for you? Or just 3 sales at £50 and no follow on sales?

If you have never done this exercise before, I strongly recommend you do so, before you start any marketing campaigns. Use the table on the next page to jot your own figures.

Going through this process is a real eye-opener. A surprising number of business owners are astounded by the figures they calculate.

Incidentally, if you are saying to yourself: "What about my overheads? My staff costs? etc.," I suggest you bear in mind these are fixed costs that do not fluctuate if you sell more or less of your product or service. In fact the more you sell the less proportion of the fixed costs would apply to each transaction.

Your life time value calculation should only take into account any <u>direct costs</u> you incur in order to satisfy the supply, in this case the cost of buying the goods.

Workshop: Calculate Your Customer's Life Time Value

Complete the table below to calculate the life-time value of your average customer. If you have different product or service lines carry out this exercise for each one.

	£
Average Value of Transactions	
Gross Margin (Profit) for Average Transaction	A
How Many Times Does the Customer Buy/Year	B
Total GP / Customer / Year [A x B]	C
How Many Years Does the Customer Keep Buying	D
Total Life Time Value of Your Ave Customer [C x D]	

Chapter 4

Treat People as Individuals to Get Glorious Responses

Have you noticed how some sales letters seem to 'hit the spot' and others just leave you cold? With some letters you can see straight away what they are getting at, and yet, others don't seem to make any sense.

Chances are, if you showed the letter that appealed to you to other people you'd get some who, like you, appreciate exactly what is meant. Others look at it from a different angle and, would perhaps, be completely unaffected by it.

This is because people *are different*. We all see things from our own point of view and have our own preconceived ideas. We all have our own beliefs and our own experiences, which influence us every day.

All this background, which we have as individuals, colours what appeals to us.

This makes it very difficult for you to write in such a way that everyone reading your letter, or advert, understands immediately what you are trying to put across.

There is a 'scientific approach' to writing adverts and sales letters that increases your chances of getting the reaction you want, as described in these pages. You can use this methodology to increase your success rate.

3 Key Actions Your Sales Letter Must Achieve...

Start your letter off in a way that captures your reader's interest. Continue in a fascinating and informative way to draw him through every sentence, paragraph and page.

Use a captivating headline or opening sentence; descriptive words and, where appropriate, the right pictures, with captions. These all impact on the response you get.

In essence your sales letter must take these three actions:

1. Seize your prospect's attention. If you do not 'stop him or her in their tracks' so they take note of what you are writing about, you won't get a result.

2. Sustain interest by focusing on the result of using your product / service.

3. Compel your reader. He must be so caught up in what you are telling; he can't resist taking the action you suggest. If your reader does not take favourable action, your letter has failed.

Use the Right Language to Cut Through Communication Barriers

The *language* you use in your letter or advert is very important. This is because we all have a language base - ways of expressing ourselves that makes sense to us. When other people use the same language as we do, we find we have an affinity with them and sometimes we seem to 'just click'.

When you offer ideas or suggestions in a conversation you hear some people say *"I **see what you mean"***, whereas someone else says *"**That sounds about right"***, whilst another responds *"**That feels good"***.

In all three sentences each person is indicating he/she has understood whatever you proposed, but each has phrased his/her thoughts in a way that feels natural to him/her.

There are visual people - these often use phrases with a visual connotation like *"**I get the picture"***. Using *'picture'* words helps them to *see* your point of *view* and *visualise* the outcome.

People who talk about things *"**sounding OK"*** are more auditory - they *hear* the ideas and can *tell* if the proposal is a *sound* proposition. They are happier with sound-based words and phrases.

Kinaesthetic people are more in touch with their feelings, and make comments like *"**I get your drift"***. They are more *comfortable* when they can relate to the ideas being *floated*. Their natural appreciation is for language containing words that create the *feelings* they want to enjoy, whether it is *security*, *comfort* or a *stress free* situation.

Capture the essence of these communication styles in your writing and you'll' achieve rapport with a greater number of people. Use a mixture of the words so you connect with *all* the different people who are reading your letter.

Here are some words, in the different language bases, you can use when writing your letter:

Visual	*Auditory*	*Kinaesthetic*
See	Hear	Safe
View	Listen	Touch
Picture	Harmony	Comfortable
Look	Noise	Explore
Observe	Rings a Bell	Fast
Watch	Heard	Handle
Vision	Discordant	Grip
Spectacle	Music to my	Feel
Imagine	ears	Floated
Visualise	Sound	Security
Appear	Tell	Stress
Show	Harmonize	Comfort
Dawn	Tune In / Out	Grasp
Reveal	Be 'All Ears'	Get Hold Of
Illuminate	Be Heard	Slip Through
Imagine	Resonate	Catch On
Clear	Deaf	Tap Into
Foggy	Mellifluous	Make Contact
Focused	Dissonance	Throw Out
Hazy	Question	Turn Around
Crystal	Wavelength	Hard
Blind	All Greek	Unfeeling
Light	Mumbo-	Soft
Colours	Jumbo	Smooth
Dim	Loud and	Scrape
	Clear	

Do be careful how you employ the different language based words - your letter must still flow and make sense to the reader.

Do remember, although we all have our preferred language we use words and phrases from the other bases as well.

When I first got involved in sales, which led to my professional writing career, I remember being told to *"paint the picture* in your sales presentation"; describe how your prospect would use your product or service, what they would see or hear, how they would feel, as in this example of a car salesman talking to a busy, important company director:

'Imagine - you look out of your office window on a cold, wintry day. Snow is falling and is already settling in a crisp, white blanket on the ground. The temperature is still dropping. You have to drive over to see a prospective client.

A big contract depends upon you getting there on time.

You smile as you say to yourself "I'm glad I bought the XYZ four-wheel drive last week."

You walk out to the car park; all sound is muffled by the snow lying on the roads, trees and bushes surrounding your offices. You open the car door and slide into the luxurious, soft cream leather seat. The door closes, whisper quiet, matching the peaceful ambience created by the snow.

You switch on the ignition. The engine gives a quick roar as you blip the accelerator. A touch of a button and you feel the warmth permeating through the seat. The powerful, smooth wipers glide across and quickly clear the front and rear screens.

As you slowly pull away you can sense the sure grip and traction of the tyres crunching across the snow. The halogen lamps cut a swathe of light through the curtain of falling snow.

The whisper of the engine gives the promise of

the power and control at your finger tips.

Suddenly, a cat runs across in front of you and you stamp on the brake. The car stops immediately, smoothly, no sliding or skidding. The ABS braking system working exactly as you expected based on what you were told when you were thinking about buying.

You relax, content in the knowledge that you will have a swift and safe journey to the appointment with your prospective client. <u>This</u> car is not going to let you down.'

This description of the result the Director enjoys uses all the base senses to create the greatest amount of rapport, regardless of the base preference of the reader.

Let's go through and identify how the base words have been weaved into the 'story'.

I've used the initial letter, before the word, to indicate the 'sense' being used.

[v] - Visual
[a] - Auditory
[k] - Kinaesthetic (Feeling)

I haven't marked *all* of the words used, just enough to give you an idea of how it works - as you go through you will recognise others:

'Imagine; you [v] look out of your office window on a [k] cold, wintry day. Snow is falling and is already settling in a [a] crisp, [v] white blanket on the ground. The [k] temperature is still dropping.

You have to [k] drive over to see a prospective client. A big contract depends upon you getting there on time.

You smile as you [a] say to yourself "I'm glad I bought the XYZ four-wheel drive last week."

You [k] walk out to the car park; all sound is [a] muffled by the snow [k] lying on the roads, trees and bushes surrounding your offices. You open the car door and slide into the [k] luxurious, soft [v] cream leather seat. The door closes, [a] whisper quiet, matching the peaceful [k] ambience created by the snow.

You switch on the ignition. The engine gives a quick [a] roar as you blip the accelerator. A touch of a button and you feel the warmth permeating through the seat. The powerful, smooth wipers glide across and quickly [v] clear the front and rear screens.

As you slowly pull away you can [k] sense the sure grip and traction of the tyres [a] crunching across the snow. The halogen lamps [v] cut a swathe of [v] light through the curtain of falling snow.

The [a] purr of the engine gives the promise of the [k] power and control at your finger tips.

Suddenly, a cat [v] runs across in front of you and you [k] stamp on the brake. The car stops imme-diately, smoothly, no sliding or skidding. The ABS braking system working exactly as you expected based on what you were told when you were thinking about buying.

You relax, content in the knowledge that you will have a swift and safe journey to the appointment with your prospective client. This car is not going to let you down.'

Notice this is written in the present tense so the reader (or listener) is 'in the scene' and is experiencing the result as it is described.

Tell Your Reader What _They_ Want to Know

In addition to this you must make sure you concentrate on your reader. Whilst writing, ask yourself "What does my reader _really_ want to know about?"

Does he/she _honestly_ care about how long your company has been in business? Or what you are trying to achieve. Statements like:

"We had a good result at the last exhibition and we would like to make this one even more successful. Which is why..."

does not interest him. He doesn't care! Always write from _his_ point of view.

One thing we all have in common as human beings is we are very interested in the result _we_ get. How whatever we purchase can _help us_. **"What's in it for me?"** is the question you are answering for your reader as you write. When you write your sales letter - does it clearly explain what result they get?

Remember, use present tense language when you describe the results they get, so they are 'in the moment' and experiencing what you portray in their imagination. It's true people buy on their emotions. The logic comes later.

But it doesn't matter how wonderful your letter is, how exactly matched your language is, how powerful your explanation is if you are writing to people who are not interested in what you are offering.

Make sure the people you are sending letters to or the publication you are placing your advert in is targeted and likely to give you the highest result (See _Careful Targeting - Creates Awesome Results;_page 27).

Workshop: 'Paint the Picture'

1. Describe the result your prospect enjoys when he/she takes up the offer you defined in the Chapter 2 Workshop.

2. Describe using picture phrases;

3. Describe using sound phrases;

4. Describe using kinaesthetic phrases.

5. Now, re-write using all 3 language-based words so your description creates rapport with as many people as possible.

Chapter 5

Careful Targeting - Creates Awesome Results

You've probably heard the normal response to any bulk mail out in business ranges from 0.5% to 1% - any more is regarded as a very good result.

This is usually because letters are sent to an unqualified list of names and contacts and is not targeted. It's like taking a handful of seed, scattering them on the ground and hoping some take root before being eaten by the birds.

'Preparing the Ground'

You have to 'sow' your seeds in prepared ground and nurture them to increase the chances of growth. The same applies to the letters and adverts you send out.

The majority of business people attempt to find new business by mailing or advertising to everyone *they think* needs their services.

It's what I call the 'scattergun' approach. The hope is their message gets *some* response - but it is rarely very productive. Hence the 1% or less figure I quoted.

Target Your Audience and Make a Real Difference

By comparison, when you target your prospects, you can get glorious results. Make sure you only write to people who have expressed an interest, bought something similar or in some other way demonstrated your product or service may be appropriate for them.
Let me demonstrate what I mean:

One of my clients is the proprietor of a letting management agency. He wanted to find new landlords. A new, luxurious development of residential apartments was being built locally.

We knew the people purchasing were very wealthy and were buying the property, in the main, as second properties for investment.

We didn't know how many were buying with the intention of letting, but there was a good chance it would be a high proportion.

We sent a letter to the people who had placed a deposit on an apartment. This was a <u>very small and very targeted list</u>, just 43 people.

The letter went out the week before Christmas.

Now, most people would say it's not good timing to send a letter just before Christmas. But I figured it was likely the people on our list would be taking a break over the Christmas and New Year period. And there was a pretty good chance they would get bored and would read the letter.

We had 2 responses between Christmas and New Year.

After New Year we sent a postcard as a follow-up to the letter reminding them about it and giving the essence of the offer again.

The final response from this highly targeted audience was a massive 44.19%. My client offers a very professional and personal service and he was able to convert 68.42% of the responses into actual clients who 'signed up' before the development was even finished!

(This rate of response and conversion is highly unusual – a percentage of 4% - 5% would normally be regarded as an excellent outcome. *But it does show how precise targeting can increase your results **dramatically**.)*

So, make sure of your target audience and prepare properly. It is crucial to your success.

'Preparing' for your mailing campaign means identifying people or businesses who have already bought or expressed an interest in what you have to offer.

'Preparing for an advertising campaign' means researching the readership of the publication you plan to use and making sure it reaches the right audience for you. (See the *27 Questions to Prepare You for Writing* on page 151).

How Do I Find My Target Audience?

Well, in the case of a mail shot, it depends upon where your prospects' details come from in the first place. If they are in your database, you have spent time building from the contacts and customers you have accrued over the years, then you have made a note of what he/she has purchased previously and what other things would interest him/her - *haven't you?*

If you don't have a database of contacts then you need to get people to qualify themselves by responding to an offer.

Let's say you've rented a mailing list of 2000 addresses. You qualified as much as you could when you sourced the list, types of business, contacts within the business, geographical location etc.

Ideally you would prefer a list specifically identifying those businesses that have bought or enquired about similar items or services to what you offer – but the information is not easily available to you in the UK. So you need to filter this list. And the only way you're going to do it is by getting the contacts to <u>tell you</u> they are interested.

How do I find people interested in my product or service?

Make an offer that elicits a response and so clearly identifies their interest.

It could be a FREE report giving valuable information that interests your prospect and has some connection with your main product or service.

If you're aiming to get people to attend a seminar then a FREE taster may be the right 'carrot' to entice your prospects.

Remember you want *qualified* contacts. You should not be looking to make a significant profit at this stage.

If you have a range of products then you could offer something at a 'silly price'. Let your prospect buy at cost or even below cost price. Once they have purchased you can nurture them into buying more from you at your normal profitable price. (Review *Know What Your Customer is Worth* on page 13).

This is the principle the book clubs work on. They take a distinct loss at the start of the buying relationship; then rely on recouping any losses and gaining additional profit from subsequent sales.

You can employ the same tactics and gain brilliant results.

Keep in mind finding your prospect is a 'numbers game'. You need to reach high volumes in order to gain a significant response. But they must still be targeted as far as possible.

Let your prospect enjoy the experience of using your product or service at a highly favourable price and you encourage him/her to spend more with you subsequently.

So, the key is to get people to self qualify themselves for your main product or service by responding to your offer.

In fact, test your different offers by sending letters out to samples of your 'database' before mailing to your whole list. Then mail to *everyone* on your list using the one receiving the highest response.

5000 is the ideal number to test. You get a result more likely to be representative of what happens when you write to the complete list.

If you don't have the budget for testing on 5000, or your list of targeted people is much smaller, carry out a test on smaller numbers.

Now you have a list of qualified people, who have effectively 'held up their hand' by requesting a copy of your free report or a place on your taster sessions or by taking up your ridiculously low-priced offer. Transfer these details to your own contact management system (database) so you can monitor every time you send out a letter or offer and the response he/she has made.

If you do not have your own database properly set up I'd recommend finding a simple CMS (Contact Management System) to get started. There are many different ones available so do check you can store everything you want to know and, more importantly, can easily access that information when you need it.

Workshop: Preparing Your Contact Database

1. Check your existing list of contacts.

2. Does it have all the information you need to qualify what each prospect is interested in?

3. If you do not have your own contact list what can you offer to a mailing list to get people to self-qualify?

4. List at least 10 different offers or approaches you can use to get people to respond to a letter from you.

Chapter 6

8 Tips to Create High Performance Sales Letters...

There are a lot of acronyms used within marketing circles to help us to remember important aspects of our activities.

One of the most frequently used is **AIDA**.

AIDA stands for:
>   Attention
>   Interest
>   Desire
>   Action

Include these 4 elements in any marketing material, whether advert, brochure, website or letter.

Start your letter by getting the readers **Attention**. Then create interest in your offer, follow by building up a desire for what you are offering.

Finally, clearly state the action you want your prospect to take.

When writing letters I use what I call an 'Extended-AIDA'. It has an extra 'A' at the end - which also stands for Attention. This Attention is the P.S., which can also attract and encourage your prospect to read your letter.

Always write your letter with the AIDA-A acronym in mind <u>and</u> focus on your prospect's point of view. Include these 8 elements in your letter and you increase the response you get:

1. **Headline** – spend the majority of your time on this. It is the ATTENTION part of the AIDA-A acronym. Include attention grabbing words already proven to be key to getting a positive reaction from readers. (See *Your Headline Can Make or Break Your Results...* on page 51).

2. **Promise** - follow up on what you promise in your headline to keep your reader's interest. If you promise some key information, tell him what it is. If your headline offers a critical report – tell him what the report contains and how it can help him. If you are making a special offer tell him more about why the offer is a good one for him. This keeps your reader's INTEREST.

3. **Offer** - Describe exactly what you are offering, what it does for him, how he benefits. If there are a number of steps to a process describe exactly what you are going to do for him – in fact, start to create his DESIRE.

4. **Testimonial** – people respond to other people's experiences and recommendations. The human nature of 'I want that too!' comes into play. Make sure your testimonials are descriptive and identify the problem your customer had or the result he wanted and the solution or outcome your product or service provided. Do this and you keep your reader's DE-

SIRE high. He wants to know more.

5. **Lose** – It is your job to make sure your reader cannot possibly ignore your offer. Make absolutely sure he understands exactly how much less his life is if he does not respond to your amazing proposition.

You would be harming him by not doing everything possible to clearly show the loss he would experience. So tell him what he forfeits if he doesn't respond. How he misses out on key benefits or results, *how his life will never be the same again...*

OK, so I'm exaggerating, but I'm sure you get the picture. People buy on emotions and use logic to justify their decisions. You need to appeal to their emotional wants and desires – the detail you provide helps them justify the logic of buying from you. (See *Use the Right Language to Cut Through Communication Barriers* on page 18).

It also reassures them *after* they have placed an order.

If we didn't buy on emotion, people would never buy expensive cars, designer clothes or larger houses. After all a small, cheap car gets you from A to B, just as a more expensive car would.

"Ah, but" I sometimes hear "it isn't as comfortable, reliable etc." That's our logic justifying the emotion of owning and enjoying being seen in a high status, luxurious car rather than an old rusty tincan. (By the way – I agree, the more expensive car *is more* comfortable and reliable).

This is still part of the DESIRE – they desire *not to lose* what you have already created an interest in.

So, having 'depressed' your reader with what

he might lose if he doesn't take up your offer, now ...

6. **Repeat the benefits** – raise the desire again to own or experience your service / product. Get your reader excited about what he can expect. Make him anticipate the result he gets from you.

And then...

7. **Action** – tell him *exactly* what to do now. Tell him to send the completed request form in the envelope provided; tell him to call the Freephone number and place his request NOW; tell him to send the email confirming his interest.

    Don't let him 'cool off'. Lead him through the steps he needs to take immediately.

8. And finally add the **P.S.** – your second headline. Having spent so much time preparing your main headline you have already discovered your second strongest – which is a natural P.S.

    This is the ATTENTION at the end of your letter. It either entices your prospect to read after he has first opened it, or re-affirms the beneficial result he receives when he responds to your offer.

    Draw him into your letter with your P.S. It too, must be compelling. State your main offer in a different way, or repeat the 'risk-free' guarantee or describe the result he enjoys.

Chapter 7

Long Letters Don't Work - *Do They?*

It amazes me; so many people quote this - *"people are too busy to read long letters"* - without any proof of what they are claiming. And yet, time and time again I - and other experienced, professional business writers - have proven the exact opposite.

So why do people have this fixed idea that short, cryptic letters are more successful than longer explanatory correspondence? It's one of those marketing myths everyone seems happy to accept - because they don't know any different.

When you write to someone, whether he is an existing client or a new prospect, your purpose for writing is because you *want him to respond.* And skilful Direct Marketing experts tell you long letters *are necessary* to give your reader the whole picture.

It is *your* job to make the letter as interesting and spell-binding as possible. It is only long, boring letters that don't work.

The Key? Your Letter Must be Plausible...

I recall a lady by the name of Tina, who is the PR & Events Organiser for a Chamber of Commerce. She looks after any mailings going out to her chamber members. One of my clients was sending an invitation (a 5-page letter) out to the members and I was discussing the project with her.

She said "I don't think long letters work; they certainly don't for me." I was intrigued and asked her why. During our conversation I discovered her only experience of long, direct-response letters was a couple of examples she had seen go out before.

Interestingly it wasn't the length that really put her off - it was the content and style of the letters.

"When I started to read through," she explained "the letter was talking about additional bonuses people would receive when they took the offer up. But the value the writer claimed for the bonuses was out of all proportion compared to the offer itself. I just didn't believe it!"

What Tina was really saying was the credibility of the letter, and therefore the writer, was suspect.

I was interested to discover if she would still feel the same way about another example - the letter my client was sending out - so I asked her to read it.

"Oh, that's interesting!" she commented as she started to browse. By the end of the first page she was amazed to find this was something of real benefit to her and she decided to ask her CEO if she could attend the seminar herself.

"I found the letter more believable because the bonus you're promising is relevant to the offer itself and the value is plausible." she explained "It was more interesting as well 'cause it described how it would help me with my work."

Be careful, if your offer seems 'too good to be true' people won't believe it and won't respond.

Make your letters compelling for all types of people

More and more research is showing us people are very different. But sometimes we forget not everyone thinks the same way as we do.

You get a person who is highly self-motivated and can see 'the big picture' and only needs to listen to a short overview to grasp what is needed. This is the person who you *might think* would prefer a short, to-the-point, letter quickly explaining the benefit and results of what you are offering.

Then you get the person who is methodical, more reserved and cautious, who wants to know *all* the pro's and con's of your offer. These people like the detail and, as you would expect, definitely appreciate a longer letter describing what you are offering, how it works and - most importantly - what it does for him/her.

And you reach some people who waver between the two extremes.

So how are you going to satisfy all these different types of people?

You may not know the person you are writing to, personally, so how can you know what type and length of letter is going to suit them? Does this mean you are going to alienate up to two-thirds of your readers if you send a long letter?

Absolutely not!

Expand the Storyline...

Let me dispel a myth about direct response letters: **short is <u>not </u>best**.

"The more you tell (factually) the

more you sell"

John Caples

If the person you are writing to is attracted to your offer she wants to know as much as possible about it, so she can make an informed decision. *If it does not appeal to her it doesn't matter how short or clever your letter is – it won't get a qualified response.*

Even people who you think would prefer short letters read longer ones *if* it is talking about *them* and what *they* get.

A short letter containing a minimum number of words is like putting a gag on your best sales person 30 seconds after they get to an appointment with an important prospect.

You wouldn't stop your salesperson explaining about your product / service, the benefits the prospect gains and how you deliver, would you?

In fact, I'd bet you expect your salesperson to demonstrate how effective your service / product is, the true benefits the prospect could expect to receive and why *your* company is the best supplier. You'd expect him/her to continue to explain until he/she is certain your prospect fully understands and appreciates the advantages proposed.

Is that right?

This is the same job your sales letter is doing – it is **'Your Salesperson in Print'.**

If you want to know what to put in your letter listen to what your best salesperson is saying. If he or she can persuade people to buy your product or service – ethically – so will your letter when you use the same explanations and informative descriptions.

*In 1905 the copywriter, John E. Kennedy, told
Albert I. Thomas:*
"Advertising is 'Salesmanship in Print'"

This is still true today.

Please remember, *every* letter you write is your 'salesperson in print' and must give the full story at all times.

Think about it for a moment - the last time you made a major purchase – did you take time to find out as much as you could about the reliability and suitability of the product or service *before* making a decision?

I recall when my husband wanted to buy a cinema 'surround' sound and DVD system, he spent *hours* pouring over reviews, internet information, specification details, comparing one make to another and then one model to another, before he made his final choice. Then he took time to consider the supplier he would use, making sure they were reliable and able to supply in an acceptable timescale.

You may think "Well, if you are spending a lot of money of course you take these precautions." However, he was spending less than £1,000, but still wanted to know everything he could find out, so he could make an informed decision he would not regret afterwards.

I'm glad to say all his research paid off. We have a very good system we thoroughly enjoy and the supplier delivered it very quickly, as promised.

Supply <u>All</u> the Facts and Figures – Good <u>and</u> Bad

Be honest with your prospect. When you approach him you can make life so much easier for him by supplying all the facts and figures, all the details he needs – both good and bad. After all, we all know it is better to buy something with 'our eyes open'.

When you tell your prospect the 'not so good' points he feels more confident about believing the good details you are describing. So, if it takes 2, 3, 16 or even more pages in a letter to explain the offer, the benefits, the downside of not taking it and all other relevant information, including anything it cannot be used for or cannot do, *that is what you do.*

The only 'cardinal sin' would be if you made your letter very boring. That is unforgivable!

So how do you avoid making your letter boring?

Surely if it is all facts and figures it's going to be boring – except for the few people who like excessive detail?

A boring letter is a trap you must avoid at all costs and it's very simple to do.

Think about the people you are communicating with and make sure you use the right language – don't be 'pompous' or 'over formal', write your letter as if you were holding a conversation with someone, be enthusiastic and write exactly as you would speak.

Writing 'As You Speak'

If you find it difficult to 'write as you would speak' because you have been educated to write correctly, with the right grammar and in full sentences, then try this little trick:

Record yourself describing your product or service to a close friend, with all the enthusiasm you can muster. Then transcribe the conversation and use it as the base of your letter.

Use Stories in Your Letter...

Use stories and incidents to demonstrate how your product or service has benefited other people and companies. Explain the challenge or problem the other people faced before buying your service or product and what you did for them.

Include testimonials from satisfied customers – not the usual *'excellent service, would recommend'*, make sure the testimonial tells what you did for them and, more importantly, what was the <u>real benefit</u> they received.

My client, who gained an impressive result in a marketing campaign, wrote this testimonial for me...

> **"It has been invaluable to have an expert writing targeted marketing material that has achieved such fantastic results – 44.2% response to a small mailing is amazing"**
> *Martin Moore, Martin & Co, Poole*

Wherever possible the testimonial should also describe the problem he was facing or solution he wanted.

How to Make Your Letter Easy to Read...

When writing your letter keep in mind the sacred rules– **What's In It For Me (WIIFM)** and **So What?**

It doesn't matter who you are writing to, everybody has one very important view point 'What's In It

For **Me**?'

Why bother to read this letter? What will I gain? What are the benefits of this offer? What problem does it solve for me?

If your letter starts off with a sentence stating how long you have been in business, the reaction from your audience might be '*So What*?' Unless you turn the statement into a tangible benefit for the reader, it is of no interest to her.

Obviously, if she already has contact with you, it may be appropriate to create confidence in your company by demonstrating its longevity. But in a first contact letter it is highly unlikely to be important to her.

Write your letter with your audience in mind. Change 'I', 'my', 'mine', 'our', etc. to you, yours – write the benefits from the reader's point of view – not from yours.

And always remember to write as if you were writing to a single person. Even if you are sending the letter out to thousands of people, only one person is reading each individual copy.

If you are not used to writing letters in this way write your letter as normal, then go through and change the emphasis, including real benefits for the reader.

Have a look at the example letters on pages 48 to 49. I received a letter written with the exact content shown in the first letter. Obviously I've changed the company and sender's details; after all I don't want to embarrass anyone!

It's written in a very formal, 'me-orientated' style – which does absolutely nothing for the reader. It offers no incentive or benefit for contacting the writer.

I have re-written it and, as you can see in the second letter, with just a few changes it has turned into something far more interesting for the recipient, and may even lead to some business in the future.

Sample Letter A:

Sample letter written in 'corporate' style
(Business name and contact are fictional)

Mr A Prospect
Any Company
Any Street
Any Town
AN0 0TH

Dear Mr Prospect,

I would like to take this opportunity to introduce myself and my
company, Huff & Puff Solicitors, to you.

Huff & Puff Solicitors have been established since 1937. We have
a large team of professionals covering a wide range of commercial
law from employment through to commercial property.

I would be pleased to explain the different services we offer and
trust you will call me if you need our advice and help.

Yours sincerely,

I. G. O. Trong
Partner

Sample Letter B

Mr A Prospect
Any Company
Any Street
Any Town
AN0 0TH

Dear Mr Prospect,

One Legal Slip Could Cost You Thousands of Pounds

There are so many different aspects of business where you have to be sure you are acting within the law. This can include employment law, contracts with other businesses and when you are renting or purchasing commercial property. Not doing so can damage your professional image as well as your bank balance.

At Huff & Puff Solicitors we understand how crucial understanding and working within the law is for a business such as yours.

You can be sure any decisions you make will not expose you to unwelcome litigation when you use our advice. Our large team of professionals covers a wide range of commercial law from employment through to commercial property.

You are welcome to take advantage of the FREE half-hour consultation we offer to discuss anything causing you concern. You will not be obliged to take our services following this meeting, although we do hope the good guidance we offer will give you the confidence to do so.

I look forward to meeting you.

Yours sincerely,

I. G. O. Tright
Partner

Workshop: Gather Your Material

Find as many examples of the results your customers have received as a result of using your product or service.

Collect all testimonials you have received from your customers, solicited and unsolicited.

If you have any good, descriptive testimonials describing a problem and how you resolved it with your product or service, get permission from your customer to use it in your marketing material.

Chapter 8

Your Headline Can Make or Break Your Results...

Write your letter in a way that grabs your prospect's attention and entices him/her to take up what you are offering.

The structure of your message, whether it is by email, letter, advert or even telephone, whether it is to entice or give the main offer, must start with a powerful headline. A strong one that appeals to your reader.

But the most important thing to remember when creating your headline is <u>what interests **you** may not attract your audience</u>. A strong headline for you may not cause even the slightest ripple of attention for others – and what appeals to them may have no substance in your eyes.

Try this little exercise...

Write 4 or 5 headlines for your product or service you think work. Now, ask 4 or 5 people, preferably not family or close friends, to place the headlines in order of preference.

I think you'll find it is highly unlikely everyone has placed them in the same order.

I did a similar exercise when I was working on a

joint venture with a business colleague. We both wrote over 50 headlines. We combined the two lists and, independently, chose the ones that appealed most to us.

We ended up with a list of 26 headlines to 'fine-tune' - but not one was repeated. Out of the 100 we had not made the same choice of a single headline!

And that was just <u>two people</u> making a selection. Imagine if 4 or 5 people were choosing!

Don't be satisfied with the first headline you think of and, when you have found a few headlines that seem to make sense; test, test and test again.

The Last Headline Often Proves To Be The Winner...

Most marketing books about direct mail tell you to write as many headlines as possible for any marketing message – up to 100 is advised by many experts.

When I first heard this, quite a few years ago, my reaction was probably the same as yours is now – *"How? Writing 2 or 3 is enough of a struggle, how can I possibly write 100!"*

Well, as with any large project you create a system and break it into smaller tasks. Be creative and brainstorm with colleagues – let them act as a catalyst for you. *Oh, and by the way, don't go for 'clever, but obscure' headlines* – leave that to the larger organisations who can afford to waste their money on entertaining mail shots or advertising campaigns.

What should your headline contain? How should it be phrased?

Get the Appeal Right and Your Reader Responds...

When you write a headline describe your offer or the result the reader can expect to gain. Always concentrate on what appeals to the reader.

People are attracted by certain appeals - they are only interested if your headline offers a real motivation for them to continue reading.

Here are just a few of the appeals to keep in mind when creating your headline. People want to:

- Satisfy their curiosity
- Be successful - in life or in business
- Be comfortable
- Make their work easier
- Gain recognition or praise from their peers or superiors
- Save money
- Make money
- Satisfy their ego
- Gain self-respect
- Be fashionable
- Be a recognised expert
- Protect themselves, their family & their possessions
- Protect their reputation
- Avoid embarrassment
- Save time
- Gain status through possessions
- Get a bargain
- Get something for free
- Protect the environment
- Prevent or relieve boredom

- Get ahead - in their career or social status
- Enjoy beautiful items
- Be popular
- Be their own boss
- Enjoy leisure pursuits
- Gain better health
- Become fit
- Get rid of aches and pains
- Be sexually attractive
- Satisfy their own sexual desires
- Gain knowledge
- Be good parents
- Relax - with friends or alone
- Be safe and secure
- Live longer
- Enjoy their life more

Use These Words in Your Headline to Substantially Increase Readership...

You have less than 10 seconds before your letter is consigned to the waste paper basket.

Use '*attention*' words and phrases in your headlines to catch your reader's eye and interest.

Including these 'attention grabbing' words in headlines has been proven to increase the chance of people being intrigued enough to read further by up to 69%.

79 'Attention' words & phrases to draw your readers in...

Here are 79 'attention' words and phrases you can weave into your headlines or opening sentence:

- Free
- Bargain
- Now
- Improved
- Introducing
- Just Arrived
- Save
- Break Through
- Send No Money
- Bonus
- Gift
- Valuable
- Priority
- Unique
- Rush
- The truth about..
- You / Your
- Miracle
- Easy
- Hurry
- Today
- How to...
- At Last
- Limited
- Opportunity
- Yes

- Caution
- Secrets
- Never Before
- It's Here
- New
- Amazing
- Win
- Last Chance
- Announcing
- Guaranteed
- Discount
- First Time Ever
- Special
- Instantly
- Discover
- Forever
- Premium
- Why
- Who Else
- Which
- Wanted
- This
- Suddenly
- Startling
- Sensational
- Quick
- Remarkable
- Powerful

- Offer
- Magic
- Incredible
- Here / Here's
- Greatest
- Compare
- Challenge
- Bargain
- Advice
- These
- Love
- Phenomenal
- Revealing
- Successful
- Astonishing
- Exciting
- Exclusive
- Fantastic
- Fascinating
- Initial
- Super
- Time Sensitive
- Urgent
- Revolutionary
- Wonderful

Write a single headline for each of these and you

have a good selection to choose from. Add a few more and *you have over 100 headlines*. When you break your task into just a few headlines for each 'attention' word or phrase, it doesn't seem anywhere near as daunting as thinking of writing 100 from scratch.

You could go a step further and decide to write a set number of headlines on each day of the week – if you write just 18 headlines per day – at the end of a week you have your 100+ headlines (I'm including Saturday's here).

The beauty of doing it this way is you're unlikely to get frustrated with a mental block and, by the time you finish; some of your headlines really sparkle at you.

I've often found the real headline gems appear in the last 20 I write! If I'd only written 30 or 40, they would never have materialised.

This is an important use of your time because, once it is done, it serves you in your business for many years to come. Take the time and effort – *after all, you're investing in the future success of your business*.

Examples of headlines using 'attention' words:

Here are some examples of headlines using a few of the words from the list.

You / Your – People are interested, primarily, in anything that helps them, makes their life easier or more enjoyable.

Including the word You/Your catches attention:

"Your Investment in Pinesuites Development Could Be Worth Up To £12,960 per Year in Income"

In this headline the specific value of the income attracted interest.

| **"Do You Make These Mistakes In English?"** |

This is a curiosity headline. The reader wants to know what <u>these</u> mistakes are and if they make them. If the word 'these' had been left out the headline would not have got the good response it did.

Who Else – this is using the 'me too' principle. The offer implies someone else has already benefited and your reader could as well:

| **"Who Else Wants To Lose 10 lbs**
In 28 Days?" |

Which – using 'which' in the headline again creates curiosity – part of what makes us human is our curiosity. If the headline is asking an intriguing question, your reader wants to know more:

| **"Five Familiar Skin Troubles –**
Which Do You Want to Overcome?" |

By using the word 'which' the reader is led to consider they may have a skin problem they could get rid of.

Now – implies 'at last' here is something worthwhile or beneficial for the reader:

> ## "Now You <u>Can</u> Get a Business Loan –
> ## Even if Your Bank Has Turned You Down"

New – always a good word to use – provided what you are offering *is* new. People like new things, ideas and innovation. Curiosity makes them inquisitive:

> ## "New Offer – 27% Discount
> ## on First Order"

Bargain – everyone likes a bargain. We all like to think we have got a brilliant deal: 'A bargain':

> ## "Fantastic Bargain, 3-in-1
> ## Business Seminar at a
> ## Massively Reduced Price"

Free – although many people think this word is overused, it still attracts attention. Even though we all tend to believe there is 'no such thing as a free lunch' we are still intrigued by the possibility of receiving something without any cost to us. Do make sure what you are offering 'Free' is truly free - if there is any cost to the reader you cannot describe it as 'free'.

> ## "Free Report Reveals 54 Secrets
> ## from Marketing Expert"

How/How to – using these words implies education and information. Finding out 'how to' do or get something or 'how' something affected an outcome attracts anyone who likes to know more about what is going on. Tie this with a problem your reader may have and it is even more effective:

> **"How to Have a Cool, Quiet Bedroom –
> Even on Hot Nights"**

Hurry – creates a sense of urgency, especially if it is linked with a 'bargain' or time limited offer:

> **"Hurry this drastically reduced offer is only
> available for 10 days"**

Breakthrough – implies whatever is offered is at the 'cutting-edge' and therefore your reader would be amongst the first to benefit from the service or product:

> **"Breakthrough Business Seminar
> Gives You Key Pointers on
> Marketing, Commercial Funding
> and Handling Business Growth Effectively"**

Describe a real benefit...

> **"New system guarantees you
> lose weight permanently –
> or your money back"**

When writing your headline, think about what is

going to attract your reader.

In an advert this could be shortened to...

"Guaranteed, Permanent Weight Loss"

However, in both cases this is a 'general claim' headline, which is probably the same as many other companies would make. Neither of them really stands out.

When You Are Specific...You are Believable

By being specific in your headline you attract attention <u>and</u> make it more believable.

Don't worry if your headline is long – when you are saying something your reader has a keen interest in the length is not relevant. Split the headline into sections to make it read better if it is really long, and make the second or third parts a slightly smaller font – as in this example:

"New system guarantees you lose at least 10lbs in weight within 28 days, without exercising or starving yourself... and what's more it's permanent – or you can have your money back"

The '...' (ellipsis) at the end of the first part of the headline draws the reader on to the next statement.

By the way, as you create your headlines you find whilst 2 or 3 really stand out; others are a natural follow-on, sub headings you can use within your letter or as a P.S.

Focused headlines are more effective than obscure or 'clever headlines'

Be clear about your offer; don't use obscure or 'clever' headlines. If your reader has to think about what you mean she isn't going to bother with it and she certainly won't be encouraged to read the rest of your letter.

And don't try to 'trick' your prospect into reading your letter. Having a headline that gets her attention and then starting your letter with, *"Now that I have your attention, I would like to tell you about..."* does not work. People feel cheated and won't read any further. It may even damage your image or reputation.

In fact, tell your prospect how the offer you are making solves a problem or creates a result she likes the look of. It sounds credible and makes her feel good, which is your prime intention.

Size Matters...

Make sure your headline stands out. In an advert, up to a third of the advertising space can be taken up with the headline. For an advert, compare it against the other items in the publication, article headlines are designed to draw the reader's eye - and is what you are competing against for your reader's attention.

Occasionally you may not think it is appropriate to use a very large headline at the top of a letter, although this does catch the reader's attention very quickly.

Organisations, such as schools, government, offices, MOD and probably Solicitors, Accountants etc. are more formal institutes and probably won't respond to large, bold headlines.

Use a bold headline in the normal size font immediately under the greeting line and make absolutely sure your first sentence is riveting for them.

Gather Ideas and Examples to Inspire Your Writing...

There are many more headline appeals that work well. Look at any marketing mail you receive or any adverts catching your attention – what is it attracted you? Would other people react in the same way? Could you adopt and adapt the essence of the headline for your service or product?

Start up a 'swipe file' and collect anything; letters or adverts that appeal to you. You may discover something you can emulate.

When you are writing use your swipe file as an inspiration fund - to give you ideas and new angles you can use. Never use an *exact* copy of someone else's work - you're likely to get yourself into trouble with copyright laws if you do.

Combine Headlines to Give a Powerful Result...

Sometimes you find it works better when you to combine 2 good headlines into 1 powerful statement – as I did with...

"Find Out How You Can Avoid up to £20,000 in Fines

...Important Advice on Legal Issues for Letting Agents..."

Workshop: Create Winning Headlines for *Your* Product or Service Now

1. Write a list of benefits and tangible results your service or product provides. (See also *Benefits and Results Sell – Not Features* on page 79).

2. Write at least one headline for each attention word. And make sure it satisfies one of the appeals on page 53.

3. Select the 3 that attract you most.

Chapter 9

Make Your Offer Compelling

You've grabbed your reader's attention with your brilliant headline or opening sentence. The next step is to keep their interest. Follow up the headline with a powerful statement to encourage him/her to read on.

Aim to get your reader excited about your offer – this is where the information about it, how it's been used by others and their testimonials – does some of the work for you.

Create an image so he sees himself using your product or getting the result your service promises...

Grab Attention, Create Interest and Desire: These Lead to Action and Harvest an Excellent Response

Earlier, I told you about the letting agent who wrote to a targeted list of people who were investing in a new, luxurious property development in a prestigious location.

My client was keen to find which of these people were considering letting their new property and to offer his property management services. The development had different types of properties which would create different rental income amounts, dependent upon the letting type they opted for.

He offered a very clear benefit to his clients, but the people we were writing to had had no dealings with him and, probably, didn't even know about the services he offered.

Our job was to pique their curiosity and give them enough information to entice them to talk to my client about what his services would do for them.

The letter (reprinted on the next page) was sent out the week before Christmas (original names have been changed for privacy reasons).

The letter is focused on the reader, what he gains. It also offers some good advice. Even if he decides not to take the offer, he knows what to look for in a letting management agency.

This freely given advice is valuable for the reader because it helps him to make an informed decision. It's probably why we got such a good take up from the recipients.

A Personal Invitation from Andrew Gavin, Managing Director of Gavin Letting Agency

Dear Mr Edwins

Your Investment in Pinesuites is Probably Worth More Than You Think...

If you are considering renting out your apartment at Pinesuites you have three choices for getting a good income from your investment in apartment 18:

- Long Term Rental
- Holiday Letting
- A combination of both

Your potential monthly income could be at least £1080 for your apartment, which equates to £12,960 per year.

But, whichever option appeals to you it is important you know all the important facts you should consider before appointing a Lettings Management Agency to handle your property for you.

Long Term Rental

10 Key things you should look for in a Rental Management Company - *if you don't want hassle*

1. How quickly is your rental payment forwarded to you? (At Gavin Letting Agency this is usually within 4 working days).

2. Do they include a comprehensive rent guarantee and £50,000 legal expenses cover for the WHOLE of the tenancy not just 6 or 12 months, thus making sure you don't lose out if your long term tenant is made redundant and cannot pay the rent (We do).

3. How often do they check your property - personally? (We make personal visits and checks 5 times a year and send the reports back to you).

4. Do they offer a personal service you can trust and rely upon, even outside 'normal' office hours? That's when any questions usually crop up isn't it? (I own this company and it is my passion to give a fantastic service to you - which is why I don't switch my phones off at 5.30 p.m.!)

5. Do they have an 8-point Landlord Quality Charter, which includes all these points - and more? (Our Charter clearly states all of these

important considerations).

6. Do they carry out stringent checks on prospective long-term tenants? (We do - as described later in this letter).

7. Do they operate a competitive and cost effective fee structure? (Ask me for a quote and you can compare the value we offer for yourself).

8. Do they look after your tenant's queries? (Or are they happy to take your money but pass the hassle on to you?) We look after all queries and organise any work is needed up to a pre-agreed budget. You won't be bothered for silly things like "the heating isn't working properly"

9. Do they have a National network of office and high profile websites and structured marketing activity so they can find the right tenants for you? (We showcase properties for rent on our own website - which receives 250,000 visits per week - and on 15 other property websites. As a result of this and our other marketing strategies we let 1 property every 22 minutes, 7 days a week).

10. Does Pinesuites Development recommend them? (I have an intimate knowledge of the development and am in constant contact with the Pinesuites Developers).

If you would like this peace of mind contact me, or my office, for more details. Telephone 9999 999 9999 and ask for Gavin or return the invitation enclosed.

You are spending a great deal of money on this property and you want to be sure it remains in the same pristine condition as it will be when you complete your purchase, so , in the future, you can continue to rent out at a good price or sell it at its full market value. The way your tenants treat your property will have a direct impact on the state of your apartment - and its value.

This is why, at Gavin Letting Agency, we make absolutely sure anyone applying for tenancy is of the right calibre and matches your specifications. How do we do this? With seven very clear, stringent checks include:

Making sure they have been legally resident in this country for 3 years by checking the electoral roll.

- Checking for CCJs or a Bankruptcy history.

- Making sure they have a good Credit Score with the Credit Checking Agencies.

- Checking their employer references.

- Checking they are earning their stated income.

- Checking with previous landlords to make sure they are suitable tenants.

And also

- Checking for any attempts at fraud by making sure their application details are accurate. We do this by comparing against any other applications they have made for credit / loans or previous rented accommodation.

Taking the time to make all of these checks on prospective long-term tenants considerably reduces the risk of having any problems with tenants. We also make sure they are the type of tenant you want, for example if you tell me you don't want young children or pets in your property then we won't try to persuade you to change your mind. We'll find the tenant matches your wishes.

Because we take all of these steps you will be able to enjoy the money you will receive from your property without losing any sleep over tribulations with tenants. It will be a pleasant experience for you - not a nightmare.

Renting your property long-term is easy to arrange - contact me, Andrew Gavin, on 9999 999 9999 or return your personal invitation to explore your rental possibilities with me.

Holiday Letting

This can be the most lucrative way of earning money from your property, especially because of the location. However you need to consider the fact the summer holiday letting season is quite short and you can't guarantee your property will be fully occupied throughout the season. The correct Marketing Strategy is key to the success of this renting option. I'm sure you know as soon as Christmas is over, the advertising for holidays goes into full swing. People who want quality accommodation in a prime location (such as Pinesuites) will book early to

avoid disappointment. Your property must be marketed from early January if you want to take advantage of the next season.

You could be earning money from holiday letting deposits before you've even completed on your property!

Our marketing strategy will match the high profile of the Pinesuites development, using all aspects of marketing - including the web and multimedia presentations. We will aim to capture overseas holidaymakers as well as people based here in the UK. Most importantly we will bring the same care and attention to detail and suitability to finding people of the right profile for the holiday lets as we do to the long-term tenants. We would not, for example, let apartments to groups of young people because we want to maintain the integrity and condition of your apartment and the ambience within the whole complex for everyone's benefit.

If you are interested in Holiday Lets you need to take action NOW. It is imperative marketing starts early January otherwise you will lose the opportunity of receiving bookings for your apartment. Contact me, Andrew Gavin, on 9999 999 9999, today.

Combination Letting

You may decide this is the best option for you. Higher holiday rents in the Summer Season - although there would still be the risk the property may not be fully occupied throughout the season - and 'winter lets' or short-term tenancy at a slightly lower rent.

An advantage you may like is this, or the holiday lets option, would give you the opportunity to enjoy the apartment and use it for yourself or your family and friends when it is not booked in the summer. You would be able to experience the ambience, security, comfort and stunning views surrounding your apartment for yourself.

As with the Holiday Lets only, it is important marketing of your apartment starts immediately. Call me or send the invitation in.

By now I am sure you appreciate how important it is to engage the right Property Letting Management team, one who has a high standard of professional service and attention to detail. I am proud of the fact my current clients are very happy with the services I provide and I would be delighted to put you in touch with them so you can reassure yourself the high standards I claim are delivered.

Please send in the enclosed personal invitation for a no-obligation exploration of the possibilities for your apartment or call me, Andrew Gavin, on 9999 999 9999.

I look forward to meeting you and helping you to realise the full potential of your investment - with the least hassle.

Kind regards

Andrew Gavin
Managing Director

P.S.   Your property could create an annual income of £12,960 but only if it is placed on the rental market NOW with a quality Letting Management Agency. Don't delay and lose your potential earnings from your investment - contact me today to get everything organised.

Tell Your Reader What To Do Next...

Now you have got your reader keyed up with your letter and offer – don't let him down. Tell him the action he needs to take, the next step he must follow so he can have the promised results for himself.

Don't assume he can figure out for himself he can phone, write or send an email to you. He is a busy person – make it as easy as possible for him. Tell him to phone the 0800 number; tell him to complete the reservation or enquiry request or tell him to send an email NOW!

Emphasise the urgency of taking the next step whilst it is fresh in his mind. If he thinks "I'll do that later" it won't happen. Chances are your letter and response mechanism will get buried under all the other things vying for his attention every day.

A Guarantee Makes it Easy for Your Prospect to Buy...

Whenever we purchase something we 'take a risk' what we are buying does what we want or gives us the result we are looking for.

And, although we don't vocalise it, the question we ask is "am I getting value for my money, will I regret this purchase?"

Because you believe in your service or product you are quick to reassure your customer *"Yes, you get exactly what I'm promising."* You do your best to remove any doubt from his/her mind.

One way you can do this is by using 'risk-reversal' – give your customer reassurance when you give your guarantee 'up-front'.

Tell your customer you give a 100% money-back

guarantee; take the risk off their shoulders gives him the confidence and peace of mind to go ahead.

I was explaining this to a client of mine, who is a business coach. She was very concerned about doing this and in fact said she found the whole idea of offering a money back guarantee, up-front, 'very scary'.

I asked her what she would do if a client of hers was unhappy with her service, would she give them a refund or say "tough!" She quickly exclaimed "Oh, I wouldn't want my client to be unhappy - and if I couldn't sort it out, of course I would refund immediately!"

"Well, where's the difference?" I queried "As an ethical businesswoman you would treat your client decently. Why not tell people at the beginning so they are reassured, rather than 'crossing that bridge' when you come to it?"

Increase the Business You Attract - Tell Your Prospect about Your Guarantee 'Up Front'

Many businesses are concerned about giving guarantees because they think people take advantage. Most people genuinely want to do business and gain the result you are describing.

Experience has shown the attrition rate rarely reaches even 5%. So, if offering a risk-reversal guarantee increases your results by, let's say 45%, even if you do have an unexpected 5% attrition you have still gained 40%. 40% more business you wouldn't have had without the guarantee.

Provided your service or product <u>does</u> perform as you claim, your customer is happy and won't even think of asking for a refund.

The 'puppy-dog' appeal

The intention behind a 100% money-back guarantee is to reassure your prospect. You can go a step further by telling your prospective customer they can have the product and not pay *until they are satisfied*.

This is the essence of the 'puppy-dog' appeal any professional salesperson knows about. It is based on the premise when someone has used or experienced the product they rarely want to give it back at the end of a trial period.

In the 'puppy-dog' story a father is looking for a puppy for his daughter's birthday. He is concerned the puppy is healthy and is the right type of breed and temperament for his little girl.

He visits different breeders to check what's available and to find out more about dogs in general; he is seeking advice from the experts.

He gets varying degrees of help from the different breeders, most of them give helpful information but, at the end of the day, they say "it's up to you what you choose" and give very little reassurance he'd be making the right choice.

Eventually he finds a breeder with some lovely, healthy puppies and one in particular catches his eye.

When he expresses his concern about whether it is right for his daughter the breeder says "I understand how you feel. I have young children myself and appreciate you want a puppy she'll love and who'll be a good companion for her as she grows up."

"Tell you what I'll do; you take the puppy and enough food for a month. Let your daughter get to know the puppy. You'll be able to see if she's as happy with it as you expected and, more importantly, you can reassure yourself that the novelty doesn't wear off" he suggested.

"After a month I'll call you. If your daughter is still happy with the puppy and it has settled in OK, you can keep the puppy and pay for it then. If she's lost interest or things just haven't worked out, I'll collect the puppy and you won't owe a penny" he continued.

The father was delighted with this arrangement and - guess what? Yes, taking the risk of buying away from the father made it easier for him and he was more relaxed about taking the puppy. Of course, by the time a month had passed the puppy was an integral part of the family and they certainly were not going to give it up.

This 'risk reversal' process is still used in business today. For example many companies who supply office spring water coolers offer a 2-week free trial period.

People like to be reassured. Give your prospects peace of mind. Take away the risk and make it easy for them to buy and you can't fail.

Workshop: Decide Your Risk Reversal

In the Chapter 2 workshop you wrote down your guarantee.

How can you improve the guarantee you are offering your prospect?

How can you make your offer irresistible?

Chapter 10

Outline of a Successful Letter

Busy people often 'scan' through a letter that has attracted their attention – they want to gather the essence of the content and offer so they can make an instant decision;

"*Is it interesting enough to read through or shall I just dump it?*"

If your offer is strong and very relevant they may read through all of it. People who <u>are interested</u> in your offer, and who like detail, may well read *every single word* of your letter, provided of course it is not boring.

Other people, who are not so 'detail orientated', read as much as they need to understand exactly what is being offered, how it benefits them – what it does for them – and what it costs.

They may not read every single word after they've gleaned the relevant detail – and this is where your sub-headlines help because they draw your reader into the important sections he/she also needs to be aware of.

Either way, to be successful, your letter has to marry with both types of reader.

To help me do this I often create a 'skeleton' or outline of my letter and offer and then 'flesh it out' with more detail, anecdotes, examples, testimonials, facts and figures.

Creating your 'skeleton outline' also helps you to be clear on what you are going to include in your letter and how you are going to make your offer 'come alive' for your reader.

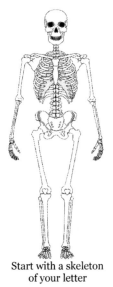

Skull = A strong and attractive Headline

Shoulders = Opening sentence or paragraph, supporting your headline

Ribs = Sub headlines and Your Offer

Pelvic Girdle = Guarantee supporting your offer

Legs = Bonus Offer - supporting your main offer

Feet = Action; 'steps you want the reader to take'

Start with a skeleton
of your letter

Toes = Post Script

The skull or **headline** – as you already know - is the most important element of your letter.

The **neck and shoulders** 'support' your headline and are the opening sentence or paragraph of your letter. Expand on the promise you've made in your headline.

The **ribs** represent your sub-headlines and the offer itself. These give your letter its shape. Think of them as short 1-liner sentences you would put in a telegram. The gist of the offer or message can often be gleaned from these short sub headings.

Your guarantee is supporting your offer – it is your demonstration of your confidence in your product or service. It is taking away the purchasing risk from your buyer and, in your skeleton, is represented by the **pelvic girdle**.

One good way to encourage your reader to respond to your letter is to offer bonuses or a free gift. The **legs** of your skeleton are the bonus or gift you're offering your reader if they act and follow the action steps; the skeleton's **feet**.

And finally your P.S. is the **toes** of the feet; 'keeping you on your toes' - by writing a good P.S. or two.

Once you've got your skeleton, or outline, you can start to add the body to your letter; fill it out.

Benefits and Results Sell – Not Features

Concentrate on the results your reader gains, not the features of your product or service. Remember **"What's In It for Me?"**

Let me quickly demonstrate the difference between a feature and a benefit:

A company sells ¾ inch drill bits.

The feature: "These ¾ inch drills are made of pure steel for strength and durability,"

The benefit: "which means you always get a smooth, evenly bored ¾ inch hole in any material: wood, brick, concrete etc. you use it on."

The easiest way to establish in your own mind what benefit each feature of your product or service provides is to write a list of features in a column down one side of a sheet of paper. In a second column, at the top, write **"which means..."** Against each feature in your first column write, in the 2nd column, the benefit it gives.

For each feature and benefit you have listed describe an example of it 'in action' and include testimonials from other satisfied customers or clients to support your claims.

Be passionate and enthusiastic about your product or service and what it does for people. Help them to 'feel' what it is like to 'experience' your service or 'own' your product. 'Paint the picture' is a phrase often used in sales training. It is also sometimes described as **'sell the sizzle, not the sausage'**. (See *Use the Right Language to Cut Through Communication Barriers* on page 18).

Use These 13 Techniques to Make Your Letter Attractive

I've already explained longer letters; describing all the benefits of an offer, have proved to be more effective.

But a number of pages with closely printed type is very discouraging for anyone to tackle. The layout and structure of your letter can invite your prospect to read – or stop them.

Use these layout techniques to make your pages appealing to your reader.

1. Keep your sentences short. Use easy to understand, simple words. Unless you are writing to people who speak the same technical language as you do, don't use jargon. Think about how you would describe your offer if you were talking to your best friend. This is the language to use in your letter.

2. Inset the first line of your paragraphs. Although this is not the 'modern' style for letters it is actually better for your reader. Tabbed paragraphs make your page more aesthetically appealing and less daunting to read.

3. Use short paragraphs – 6 lines or less. Long paragraphs give a 'solid' appearance, which does not encourage your reader to tackle it. It is perceived as hard work and creates a barrier for your prospect. Aim to cover just one point in each paragraph.

4. Don't finish a sentence or paragraph at the end of a page. You want your reader to continue onto the next page...a split sentence or hyphenated word entices them to turn over so they can finish the word or sentence. People rarely want to stop mid-sentence!

Plain is Best...

5. Don't go overboard with fancy fonts or colours. If you are writing a letter to a friend or business colleague it's unlikely you would add colours and different fonts to your message. This is no different. You are *writing an informative letter* to your prospect or customer. Adding too much colour and large, fancy fonts throughout your letter screams 'sales letter' at the reader.

6. Use bullet points and indented paragraphs to make your points stand out. Don't be tempted to use fancy symbols for your bullets; just a simple • gives the best effect.

7. The same applies to numbered lists, use straight forward numbering

8. Make your letter as easy to read and attractive as possible. Use serif fonts for the main body text of your letter.

What is a serif font?

There are serif fonts and sans serif fonts. Serif fonts are those with a slight tail at the bottom of each letter. The 'tail' draws the eye to the next letter or word and creates a flow so there is less strain on the eye. It makes reading much easier.

Example serif fonts are:

- Times New Roman
- Century Schoolbook
- Courier (Old typewriter style)
- Georgia

What is a sans serif font?

Sans serif fonts do not have the little tail. They are a harsher font and can, almost, stop the reader in his tracks. They are sometimes used in headlines or sub-headlines when you want to catch the reader's eye. They can be used to pull the reader into the letter when they are glancing through the pages.

Be careful though, you could have the opposite effect if your prospect is already reading through your entire letter.

Example san serif fonts are:

- Arial
- Goudita Sans SF
- **Impact**
- MS Sans Serif

Link Your Paragraphs to Create a 'Flow'

9. Link your paragraphs so your letter 'flows'. These links are known as transitional phrases. They help the reader to make the 'transition from paragraph to paragraph'.

Use links such as:

- 'The thing is...'
- 'But that's not all...'
- 'Now - here is the most important part'
- 'And in addition...'
- 'Better yet...'
- 'You will see for yourself why...'
- 'So that is why...'
- 'More important than that...'
- 'What's more...'
- 'But there is just one thing...'
- 'Make up your mind to...'
- 'The secret?'
- 'Make up your mind now to...'
- 'Take advantage of this opportunity to...'
- 'Now - for a limited time only -'
- 'Here's your chance to....'
- 'So post your *request / reservation* today - while the special offer is still in effect.'
- 'That's a good question...'
- 'Think about it...'
- Interestingly enough...'

- 'To help you do this...'
- 'What you do next...'
- 'Remember...'
- 'Now - here's an added feature...'
- 'So - let me ask you...'
- 'Of course...'
- 'But first...'
- 'The Result?'

Keep It Personal...

10. Write your letter to a specific person. Have a picture in your mind of your ideal prospect or reader.

Start your letter with the person's name; "Dear John" or "Dear Mrs Allen".

When you've finished your letter, go through and replace the name of the person you've written to with someone else's. Does the letter still work? If not, scratch it and start again.

11. Next, go through your letter and replace your company name, product or service with your competitors. Is the letter describing your competition perfectly? If so – you haven't got a good working sales letter.

Your letter must have something unique or different; otherwise your prospect has no reason to buy from you rather than your competitor.

12. How does your letter read? In 'The Greatest Direct Mail Sales Letters of All Time', Richard S Hudgson suggests the 'hat test':

"Put on your hat and go out of your office and find someone who doesn't know your product or service. Ask her to read your letter aloud. Listen to the way she reads it and any questions she asks. You'll soon discover if you've got it right. If she does ask questions - you need to add more information!"

Sign Your Letter Personally

13. Always, always, always sign your letter with a hand-written reflex-blue signature. Never use a computer generated 'handwriting' font and do not get someone to p.p. your letters.

Both of these give the recipient the impression he/she is not important enough for you to take the trouble.

Why reflex-blue? Reflex blue is the closest printed blue to the Royal Blue ink used in fountain pens. Tests have proved a blue signature does raise the response quite dramatically.

Obviously, signing the letters individually in blue ink is ideal. But if you are sending out large numbers, it's not very practical. You get writer's cramp and it takes you a very long time.

How to create your own signature image...

Use a piece of white paper, make sure it is bright white otherwise you may get a slight shading effect.

Use a thick nib pen - or a felt-tip pen - with blue ink.

Sign the paper a number of times, in a larger script than you normally would, until you are happy with the result.

Scan the signature you prefer at a high resolution, about 1200 dpi. Save it as a JPEG or TIFF format graphic.

When you create your letters on your own computer you can insert the graphics in the signature position.

If you are having your letters printed your printer may ask for the signature graphic to be supplied as a separate file.

If you do not have computer equipment or a scanner you can get a design studio to create the image file for you.

Note: Do you use Microsoft® Word to write your letters?   Do you get frustrated when things suddenly happen, for no apparent reason?   Send for your Free Guide:

"How to Banish, Forever, the Hair-Tearing Frustrations of Microsoft® Word® When Writing Your Sales Letters"

See my special offer for a Free report, at the back of this book.

Workshop: Draft Your First Letter

1. Draw up 2 columns on a piece of paper. Head one **'Features'** head the other **'which means that'**.

   List all the features of your product or service and offer in the first column.

   Add the benefits and results each feature provides in the second column.

2. For each feature/benefit write a description of it in use.

3. Find a customer comment or testimonial supporting your description.

4. Review the headlines you have written and selected.

   Can any of them be used as sub-headlines throughout your letter?

5. Using all the material you have gathered and written in the previous Workshop sessions; write the first draft of your letter. Keep your words and sentences simple and short. Avoid having more than 5 or 6 lines in a paragraph.

   Use link phrases to create a flow between paragraphs.

   Include the 'attention' words as part of your descriptions.

   Include your guarantee and spell out the steps you want your reader to take.

   Finish off with a strong P.S.

6. Review your letter. Check the emphasis is on 'you - the reader'. Have you used all the base languages in order to create as much rapport as possible with your reader? (See *Use the Right Language to Cut Through Communication Barriers* on page 18).

7. Compare against '*20 Points to Make Your Sales Letter Compelling*' on page 154

Chapter 11

Design a Responsive Order Form

The 'Order Form' is your response mechanism. It is the most important piece in your mailing package. It is the final 'call to action' your prospect sees.

In many cases it can be a real stumbling block for someone and can often prevent a person from responding if it is too difficult to complete or doesn't in any way confirm he/she is making the right decision.

Make it attractive, easy to fill in and valuable looking. Confirm the main thrust of your offer and any bonuses and guarantees you have made in your letter.

Plan to spend as much time as needed to get it right.

It is your **1-page advert for your whole offer** and your reader must get the full picture from this form alone.

Avoid Simple, But Expensive Mistakes...

It is so easy to get it wrong! I recall one of the first forms I 'designed'. I was sure I'd got it right.

But the trouble is, when you have worked on something for a long time, and you've got all the details of the offer clearly in *your mind*, it's so easy to miss something that is 'obvious' to you. *And yet it can be critical to the order being placed correctly.*

In this case the 'offer' being made was for a seminar. The first place booked cost £100. Subsequent places (for colleagues) cost £75 each. The order form did not take into account someone could be booking for other people and NOT INCLUDE HIMSELF.

And the way the form read anyone else could attend for £75, regardless of whether the recipient came along as well or not. It was not clear the *first place cost £100* – whoever was attending. You can be sure I didn't make *that* mistake again!

A Form That Is Difficult To Complete Is Often Abandoned...

The most effective way to check your response form is easy to complete is to find someone who has not been involved in preparing the project. Ask her to fill in the request response. When she has finished, check if it has been completed as you expected and ask her if she found any part confusing or difficult to understand.

When you are designing your response form bear in mind people do not like 'ordering things' and often **hate** filling in forms – too much like work! So give your response form an attractive name; such as Priority Reservation, Special Enquiry or Delegate Certificate etc.

These 31 Tips Make Your Order Form Easy to Use...

- Avoid calling your form 'Order Form'. Priority Reservation, Special Enquiry or Delegate Certificate is a more gentle approach.

- Use a separate sheet of paper for your order form. It is important - make it look as if it is a valuable piece of paper.

- Do not write anything on the back of the form. It distracts your prospect and he/she may delay, and then forget, to complete and send the form.

- Put a border around the form to enhance its appearance.

- Use a heavier quality paper, 120gsm or a special paper like parchment, to give a feeling of value.

- Don't use high gloss paper - ball-point or felt tip pens smudge. Make sure the paper you use is OK for all pen types.

- Include tick boxes and Yes at the beginning of the form:

  ❑ **Yes**, I do want to...

- Restate the benefits and results your respondent can expect to receive i.e. the offer. Write the confirmation statements as if he/she were saying it. Emphasise the positive benefit, not the negative angle.

- Repeat your guarantee – to remind them him he is taking a low-risk or risk-free action. Highlighting in a coloured or shaded panel helps it to stand out so your prospect is happier about entering his details. On a fax-back form place the guarantee in a frame instead of shading.

- If your offer is time sensitive show the cut-off time on your form.

- Make the form simple to fill in and check it flows easily.

- Ask your prospect to complete your form in block capitals so you can decipher his details accurately.

- If the order is for products or places on seminars etc. allow room for a quantity to be added so he can order or reserve more than one if he wishes.

- Use crystal clear wording. Be careful what you write doesn't make any assumptions.

- Ask for full contact details, including email addresses.

- Start the contact details with Mr/Mrs/ Miss/Ms so you can address future mailings correctly, especially if he/she enters an initial rather than a first name. It also saves embarrassment where the first name could be either gender, such as 'Chris'.

- Leave enough lines for the address. Some addresses are longer than others; make sure there is enough room.

- Add a separate line for the postcode. People often forget to include the postcode in the address. Using the word 'Postcode' reminds him/her to enter it.

- Ask for permission to use the email address supplied for future offers (use a checkbox). This is a legal requirement (Data Protection Act) in the UK.

- Give an opt-out box if he doesn't want details of further offers or information from you. It helps you keep your database contact clean so you are only writing to people who are interested in what you provide.

- Give an opt-out box if he doesn't want details of offers or information from other organisations. (Especially if you want to create revenue by renting out your contact list).

- Code your form so you know which letter or headline is creating the response. In this way you can be sure which of your test mailers is the most successful.

- If payment is by cheque, tell him/her who to make the cheque payable to.

- If payment can be made by credit card or switch, leave enough room for the card numbers, expiry dates, issue date (switch), security code and signature.

- Include your postal address on the order form – in case it gets separated from the rest of your mailing package.

- Tell your respondent what to do with the completed form. Don't leave him guessing; tell him to place it, with his cheque, in the reply paid envelope you've supplied; or send it to the freepost address; or fax it through to you.

- If you are using a fax-back form, do not use heavy shading – especially where he is writing his details.

It takes a long time to scan and fax and could be illegible when you receive it.

- Make sure it is the right size for going through a fax machine.

- Ask your prospect to refer a friend or colleague. By having a 'referral panel' you get new contacts for your database. When you get a referral qualify it – make sure he/she really is interested in what you are offering - before adding him/her to your list.

- Say 'Thank You' - show your appreciation for his/her business.

- Get someone who hasn't been working on the project to complete your form. If he/she has any difficulty, re-design it.

Sample Response Forms:

On the next few pages are samples of response forms following the advice I've given you in this chapter.

The first example is for a demonstration of a free colour laser printer offer that was sent out to estate agents. It clearly states the offer and benefits the prospect enjoys by responding. It describes the additional bonuses the reader gains by acting swiftly and the guarantee is shown in a separate box. *(Incidentally if this offer appeals to you I'm sure Grant Marsh, the M.D. at IC Office Solutions would be delighted to speak to you, just mention you saw his offer in this book).*

The second sample is for a priority reservation on a teleconference I held. Again it describes the benefits of taking part and the additional bonus for the people who respond quickly. This also has a section for the recipient to refer someone else who is interested in the event.

Priority Request

✓ **Yes Grant, I do want to save £5,424 on my printing costs over the next 3 years,** starting with a FREE DSc38u digital colour laser printer. And I want people to compliment me on the vivid, sharp colours in the photos on my property particulars and I want to be able to produce colour details at a 'supersonic' speed of just 2.14 seconds per printed page. Please call me on telephone number: _____ to explain more about your offer & arrange a 'no obligation' demonstration of the printer by one of your qualified technicians. Call on (date) _____ am/pm (please delete as appropriate)

I understand I will also receive my FREE report; "Revealed… The 23 Marketing Secrets The Most Successful Estate Agents in the UK Don't Want You to Know!"… with the demonstration of the colour digital laser printer.

❏ I am responding within 10 days and, hopefully, I am one of the first 27 to request my demonstration of the DSc38u. If I am, and I decide to take up your offer after the demonstration, I claim my additional bonus of a reduction in the price per colour print for the first 6 months. My reduced price will be just **8p per colour print**, giving me an **additional saving of £240** over the first 6 months.

❏ I think it's great that if I'm one of the first 27 to reply and I decide to keep the printer after the free, no obligation demonstration, I'll be given the option of keeping the price fixed for a further 2 years after the normal 3-year contract. This means I'm paying no more for my prints in year 4 and 5 than I am in years 2-3, giving me a **massive saving** of at least £960 over the final 2 years.

❏ **Yes** Grant, unfortunately, I have recently changed my printer but I expect I'll be replacing it _____ (month/year). Please make a note to contact me with your current offer just beforehand. I am also claiming my own personal copy of the report "Revealed… The 23 Marketing Secrets The Most Successful Estate Agents in the UK Don't Want You to Know!" within 10 days. Send me the report immediately so that I can start using these techniques to boost my agency results. I am enclosing a self-addressed C5/C4 envelope with 60p in stamps.

❏ Although I can see your offer is unbelievably good value –I don't want to take advantage.

100 DAY RISK FREE GUARANTEE

Even if I decide to take a demonstration of this full colour, auto-duplex, A4/A3 digital laser printer and then choose to take up your offer of having this printer supplied and installed **FREE** of charge, I will still have **100 full days** to test its quality, reliability, ease of use and cost effectiveness.

If I don't agree that this printer lives up to all your claims I can call you and have it removed immediately. All I will pay for is the actual printing I've done during the 100 days trial run.

PLEASE USE BLOCK CAPITALS:

MR/MRS/MISS/MS:		NAME:		SURNAME:	
POSITION:					
ESTATE AGENCY:					
ADDRESS:					
POSTCODE:					
TELEPHONE:		FAX:			
MOBILE:		EMAIL ADDRESS*:			

* Please keep me informed by email of any relevant future offers ❏
* I do not want to be kept informed by post of any future offers ❏
* I do not want to be kept informed by post of any offers from other companies that you believe would be of interest to me ❏

Please complete this request and pop it in the post today.

Send to:

Dept: FREE-Demo CB28
IC Office Solutions Ltd (Head Office)
Unit 14 Chatto Way Industrial Estate
Chatto Road
Torquay
Devon
TQ1 4UE

Or You Can Fax Your Request for your no-obligation demonstration, **Free**, to:

(0800) 328 5919

Thank You for requesting your no obligation demonstration of this FREE full colour A3/A4 digital laser printer

This response form starts off with a bold, benefits laden statement from the responder.

Priority Teleconference Reservation

☐ **Yes Kelly, I do want to discover the additional techniques, secrets and insights Carol Bentley is revealing in this first-time ever <u>live</u> teleconference.** During this 70-minute teleconference, scheduled for **September 20th at 6 p.m.**, Carol gives her most considered answer to my most burning question about how to write the most responsive, compelling, fascinating, attention grabbing, results generating sales letters and adverts. And I get to hear all the answers to the questions other business owners are asking that give me even more insight to how to use this magical marketing methodology. And all for the incredibly low, price of **just £37^{+VAT}**

☐ Here's the question I want answered $^{(Please\ print)}$:_____

_____

(...continue on reverse if necessary)

My email address* for Conference Details Notification: _____

☐ I really like the idea of being able to **listen again** to the teleconference afterwards so I can pick up crucial techniques and advice I might miss during the call. I look forward to receiving my **CD containing the recording of the teleconference.** There is <u>no additional charge</u> for my copy of this audio record of these powerful insights.

☐ **Quick-Action Bonus:** I'm making my reservation <u>immediately</u> and, hopefully, I'm quick enough to be one of the **first three to respond.** If I am one of the lucky 3, I claim my **additional, valuable bonus – worth up to £2,194** – of having my letter or advert personally critiqued by Carol. I understand during the 1-on-1 critiquing Carol shows me how to add 'sizzle' to my offer to make it completely irresistible to my prospects.

What's more, this includes **three private 15-minute telephone consultations** (alone worth <u>£900</u>) during which Carol goes through my letter (or advert) and gives me personal tuition, on proven and tested copywriting methodology; I learn more techniques; more phrases; more compelling terminology to apply to all my marketing material; letters, adverts, brochures, newsletters, flyers, response forms and web pages.

If I want Carol to critique a sales letter I also get her keen advice on how to create the most **magnetic response form** possible to go with it.

And I can revise and resubmit my piece for critiquing up to three times as I apply Carol's insights.

☐ Kelly, unfortunately I cannot make that date and time. But I really <u>do want to have access to this insightful and valuable information</u> so I can use it to turn my letters and adverts into <u>high-performing sales generators</u>. Although I appreciate I cannot ask my own specific question, I understand that if my request arrives quickly enough I **could still qualify for the 'quick action bonus' valued at £2,194.** Please rush me my personal copy of the teleconference CD as soon as it is available. I have access to this valuable information for the **same low price of just £37^{+VAT}**; there is no additional P&P charge.

☐ Please send an invitation to this teleconference to my colleague. $^{Name:}$ _____ $^{Email:}$ _____

PLEASE USE BLOCK CAPITALS:

MR/MRS/MISS/MS		FIRST NAME:	
SURNAME:			
POSITION:			
COMPANY:			
ADDRESS:			
		POSTCODE:	
TELEPHONE:	FAX:	MOBILE:	

* Please keep me informed <u>by email</u> of any relevant future offers ☐
I do <u>not</u> want to be kept informed <u>by post</u> of any future offers ☐
I do <u>not</u> want to be kept informed <u>by post</u> of any offers from other companies you think would interesting to me ☐

☐ I am enclosing my cheque, payable to Promote Your Business Ltd, for £43.48 (£37^{+VAT})
☐ I prefer to pay using my Credit / Debit Card and will visit **www.CarolBentley.com/teleconference** to pay online

Return this **Priority Teleconference Reservation** to the freepost address shown below. Pop it in the post today.

TEL105
Promote Your Business Ltd
FREEPOST NATW661
Swanage
BH19 1BR

This response form goes into great detail about the bonus offer as well as the main proposal. Sometimes people respond just to get the bonus!

Practice: Design Your Responsive Response Form

1. Draw up a Response form for your offer.
2. Compare what you have designed with the checklist on page 157

Chapter 12

Your Mailout Package

How _do_ You Read Your Letters?

The way people select, open and read their letters fascinate me. It is very rare letters are opened in the order they land on the desk or doormat and, unless the correspondence is from a friend or family member, the letter may not be read through from beginning to end.

In fact, when people receive their post – whether it is personal or business – they often use an unconscious selection process for the sequence they open and read it in.

The most common actions a person follows are:

He decides, probably without really thinking about it, the order in which to open items. Bulky, interesting packages are usually opened first because they create curiosity, especially if they are unexpected. These are followed by any hand-written letters, which are more personal and likely to be from a friend or relation. Next comes the 'official – looking' letters such as bank statements, government correspondence etc. Finally, if at all, the 'junk mail'.

Yes, that's what we call it isn't it? The sales letters from people who are trying to catch our attention is often referred to as 'junk mail'. And, whether we like it or not, our letters may be regarded in the same way. Especially if the person has no interest in what we are writing about because we have not targeted the right people.

When a letter is opened research has shown most people:

1. Check the name and address to make sure it is addressed correctly.

2. Read the headline or the first sentence.

3. If that has attracted his/her attention sufficiently, the end of the letter is checked to see who it is from and...

4. If there is a P.S. this is read as well. (*Always* add a *P.S. – it is your second chance to get your reader's attention and entice him/her to read your letter*).

Then the decision is made to either 'bin the letter' or read it.

It is your job to make sure your letter is read, and not thrown out, by getting every possible aspect of it right so your targeted reader responds in the way you want him to.

By the way, 'gimmicky' bulk mail only works if the recipient is interested in your offer. No amount of clever 'promotional gifts or inserts' create a response where there is no interest or desire. ***This is where targeting your audience makes a real difference.***

I regularly get a package, with a sample gift inside, from a promotional gifts company. I get 5 or 6 packages every year, and even though I have told them it is highly unlikely I'll ever place an order, they continue to send the samples - *just in case.*

I suspect their mailing list is not very targeted!

How the Package is Collated can Decimate or Raise Your Readership

Have you ever thought about the importance of how your mailing package is collated and placed in the envelope?

Do you ever consider the way items are folded and placed in the envelope could affect the response to your mailing?

It can and it does!!

Why?

Think about when you receive an offer in the post. What is the first thing you notice after opening the envelope? I'm guessing it is the first sheet of paper and whatever is on it.

You want your prospect to see something to quicken his pulse, make his eyes light up – or at least intrigue him enough to look further.

Now, the majority of your hard work has been geared towards your headline – so it must be the first thing your prospect sees.

The way you fold and insert your letter and the rest of the mailer content impacts on this.

So does the paper you use. If you use letter headed paper printed in the traditional style; large logo at the top of the page followed by address details your headline could be completely out of view.

And that's bad news because if your company name and logo doesn't offer an immediate benefit orientated result – and few do – chances are your letter won't be opened and your wonderful headline never even sees the light of day!

This is why I always recommend client's have 2

letterheads. One normal style – used to correspond with existing clients and suppliers etc. and one where the logo and details are shown discretely at the bottom of the page. When a mailing is being sent out to targeted prospects, who have no previous experience of your company, use plain paper to start your letter and use the 'bottom' header paper as the last page in the letter.

This means the whole of your first page is given over to making a very strong offer. AND your main headline or opening sentence appears on the first third of your letter, regardless of how your letter is folded:

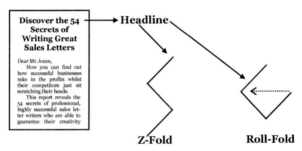

Your ideal 'package' contains:

1. Your letter describing your offer and the results it gives.

2. An introductory (lift) letter – if you are using this. A *lift* letter is a letter from a third party recommending your product or service. It can be from a satisfied customer or a recognised expert in your profession or industry. It is a longer, more detailed version of a testimonial.

3. Your Response Form (See *Design a Responsive Order Form* on page 89).

4. A Business Reply Envelope (BRE) or Freepost Envelope.

5. Leaflet or flyer about your product or offer (if appropriate).

Do make sure all the items are collated and facing the correct way. One thing you cannot be sure of is how your prospect will pull the contents out of the envelope, which way the 'package' is facing when it is extracted.

How does your letter 'appear' as it is pulled out?

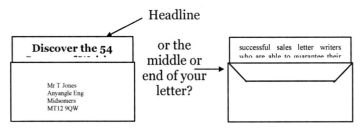

I've personally found even different size envelopes affect the way I open a letter.

If it's DL (with the letter inside folded into 3) I usually slit the envelope open with a paper knife and pull the letter out with the address side facing me.

If it's C5 (the letter is folded in half to A5 size), I usually have the back of the envelope facing me, slit or pull open the closing flap and then extract the letter. So I see the back of the contents first.

If it's a C4 envelope, containing an unfolded A4 letter, it could be opened either way.

I think I might be the direct response mailer's nightmare!

But I wonder how many other people open their envelopes in different ways?

Use DL envelopes for your sales letter. C5 and C4 are unlikely to be used for an individually written letter. You want your letter to give the impression it is personal. Make sure the content attracts attention on <u>both</u> sides of the package.

If you have carefully designed your response form to repeat the major results orientated benefit, then it can be the alternative view of your package. Fold it so your letter, with its headline, is facing in one direction – usually towards the addressed side of the envelope – and fold the response form so the major impact shows facing the back of the envelope.

Please do *not hide* your letter inside any other leaflets, brochures or forms you are placing in your package.

It amazes me how often I receive mailings where the 'letter' is at the bottom of the pile or slipped within the package so it is completely hidden from view. I could understand it if the 'top sheet' had a very strong headline or 'call to action' - but it rarely does.

Welcome to the 'Peek' Party

Have you ever slit open an envelope and just 'peeked' in to see what it contains? And then decided, in an instance, you are not interested and don't bother to take the contents out of the envelope?

You'd be surprised at how many people do just that!

When you've collated and placed the contents of your mailer in the envelope is a 'peeker' intrigued enough to pull your letter out and read what you have to say?

Test the peek view for yourself before sending your letter off.

Mailing Houses Can Save Time *but...*

If you are using a mailing house to collate and insert your items into an envelope make sure the package is being collated as you intended.

On one occasion, in my early days of creating direct response campaigns, I was horrified to discover a client's mailing house had not been assembling the package as I had instructed. Let me explain.

I'd written quite a short letter – only 4 pages – designed a flyer and response form (Priority Reservation Certificate) and an introductory lift letter from a satisfied client, which was 2 pages. The letters were printed double-sided. So, the main letter was two sheets of paper and the lift letter was on a single sheet.

I had asked for the lift letter to be facing in one direction with the main letter following behind, collated and folded together. The flyer and response form brought up the 'rear', with the response form facing towards the back – it had a strong affirmation of the offer and benefit.

Mailing houses use folding and inserting machines. And quite often these machines only pick up, fold and insert single sheets of paper. Obviously this is an easier and more cost-effective way of handling mail shots where many thousands of letters are being sent out.

I was surprised we did not get a particularly high response to this mailing. Especially considering this particular list of contacts is normally very open to offers made by my client.

When I looked into it further I discovered even though I had asked for the letter pages to be collated and folded together – as you would if you were sending an individual letter out for yourself – this had not happened.

Each page of the letter was folded and inserted

separately – and I am certain this suppressed the number of people who took up my client's offer.

Why am I so convinced? Because if you receive a letter from a friend or business associate the pages would be collated and folded together – wouldn't they?

So, if you receive a letter where each page is separated in this way, doesn't it just scream *'mail shot – sent to 1,000s of people'*?

How do you get around this?

The letters have to be collated and folded by hand. It is more costly – especially if a mailing house is doing the work.

What you need to do is satisfy yourself – as far as you can –the additional revenue you would expect to gain covers the extra expense of folding and sorting. Which is why testing is so important.

If you cannot justify (or afford) the extra cost of collating and folding by hand, and your letter is 3 or 4 pages, you could arrange to print onto A3 and get your printer to crisp fold to the size you need for the envelope you are using.

The insertion machines are able to handle the letter to go into your package and it should keep the costs down.

If your office is near a college or university and you have the room to temporarily accommodate a number of people, you could advertise for students to take casual employment and help you with the 'hand' sorting and assembling of your package ready for mailing. Although you have to supervise this activity, it could work out less expensive than using a mailing house.

Send Yourself a Letter...

The important lesson I learnt from this was to make sure I am on any mailing list used for any material I create, so I know EXACTLY what is going out and how it appears when it reaches the prospect's desk.

I strongly suggest you do the same.

After all, you have taken the trouble to write, re-write and edit your letter to make it as near perfect as you can, you've designed your response form to make it as attractive and valuable looking as possible.

And you've made sure the signature is in reflex blue – in fact you've used every trick in this book to increase the possibility of gaining the high response you want – and you don't want all your hard work cancelled out by the way the package is presented. *It is all part of your 'selling kit'.*

Of course, your mailing may be successful – in spite of the way it is inserted into the envelope – so just imagine - how much better would it be if it is presented properly, as a 'real' individually written letter?

Chapter 13

How to Guarantee Your Results

Your letter can only be counted as successful when someone actually responds and takes up your offer. Until that happens, you need to continuously refine and adjust your headline, offer and letter content.

It is crucial you do not spend a great deal of money on sending out an offer to everyone on your contact list until you are sure the way you have presented your offer creates the highest response possible.

The only way you *can* be sure is by testing.

Testing is critical to the success of your marketing, whether it is a letter, an advert, brochure, website or newsletter.

Don't spend more on testing your offer than you can afford to lose. When you test, you may get little or no response to one headline or offer and glorious results from another.

When you have a measured, highly successful response, you can be confident you will get a similar lucrative result when you send it out to everyone on your list.

For adverts, start small with classifieds, and only increase in size when the response you get is at least break-even and, preferably, profitable. If your first advert does not bring a result then stop it. Make a change you want to test and run it again.

Test Everything - Especially Your Headline

The single, most important element of your letter or advert is the headline. You've already discovered in this book how crucial the headline is to creating the response you want.

When you develop your letter or advert test the headline first.

Why?

The challenge we all have is to appreciate we see things from our own, personal perspective – and so does everyone else. The headline that appeals to you may not appeal to other people.

Throughout this book I have emphasised the importance of getting the right headline, and I **can't stress this enough**.

Let me give you another demonstration:

The following headline pairs contain ones that worked successfully and the alternative in each case which proved not to be as good. It was only through testing the successful version was established.

In many cases the headline tested as a 'first option' was the <u>least successful</u>. If testing had not been done a great many sales would have been lost.

Select the headlines from these samples that appeal to you. Then, without letting anyone see your choice, ask a few other people to do the same. Finally compare your selections with the results the advertisers themselves found (see the actual results the writers achieved at the end of this chapter).

Which of these Headlines Work for You?

a)   Advert for English course:

"The Man Who Simplified English"

"Do You Make These Mistakes in English?"

---

b)   Advert for a Book

"How to Win Friends and Influence People"

"How to Ruin Your Marriage in the Quickest Possible Way"

---

c)   Insurance Company

"Retirement Income Plan"

"What Would Become of Your Wife If Something Happened to You?"

---

d)   Property Letting Management Agency

"Quality, Professional Letting Management"

"Your Investment in *<development>* is Probably Worth More Than You Think..."

No-one's selection is wrong – everyone chooses what appeals to them.

What *you want* is the headline that creates the greatest response.

And this exercise, reiterates how important the headline is.

After testing the headline the next part of your testing sequence is to check the offer is the best you can possibly make (See *Know What Your Customer is Worth* on page 13).

Write your offer so it is really compelling. (See *Make Your Offer Compelling* on page 65).

Your job is to find the right combination of headline, offer and guarantee that attracts the highest number of people in your target market.

Monitor Your Responses

Make sure you know which letter has been successful. Code every letter you send out so when you get an answer you know which version has worked for you.

The code can be a Dept reference in the address or a printed code on a response form.

In an advert in a publication, use letters to identify the publication – perhaps the initials of the publication name and, in the case of a daily newspaper, which day of the week the advert was run.

Change the reference number for your advert every time you make an alteration – no matter how small. Do this so you always know *exactly why* your response increased or dropped.

For example, part of the postal address could be:

Dept **ST186a**

ST - is the publication, e.g. **S**unday Times

18 - is the week number the advert was placed

6 - is the advert offer or product

a - is the version of the advert.

The letter (a) is increased whenever any changes are made, no matter how small. So in this case, the second version would be **6b**.

Another way of coding your response mechanism is to use a contact name, e.g. 'Ask for Hazel'. When you get calls for 'Hazel' you know which advert version he/she is calling about.

Or add a single letter to the end of your postcode to distinguish the mail arriving in response to your letter or advert from your other post.

Whatever you use make sure you keep a tight control on what is happening so you know who to follow-up with what offers in the future.

When you've got a 'winning formula', don't rest on your laurels. Monitor the results so you know the trend. Keep your successful letter or advert as your benchmark and start to test slight alterations – remember, only one element at a time.

"Aim to continuously improve on the winning marketing pieces that are already working best for you."

These Headlines Out-Performed The Others:

a)   Advert for English course:

"The Man Who Simplified English"

*****"Do You Make These Mistakes in English?"*****

The second headline produced nearly three times the sales the first brought.

b)   Advert for a Book

*****"How to Win Friends and Influence People"*****

"How to Ruin Your Marriage in the Quickest Possible Way"

This book, which is well known throughout the world, was written by Dale Carnegie and incorporated into his training courses. The 'How to Win' headline out-pulled the other by nearly 250%

c)   Insurance Company

*****"Retirement Income Plan"*****

"What Would Become of Your Wife if Something Happened to You?"

The first headline increased response over the second by nearly 500%

d)   Property Letting Management Agency

"Quality, Professional Letting Management"

*****"Your Investment in *<development>* is Probably Worth More Than You Think..."***

The second headline, used on a direct-response letter, created a massive 44.2% response.

Workshop: Get Control of Your Responses

1. Create a response code to use for your next mailing campaign.

2. Make sure you have a database or other means of recording the contact details and code as your offer is accepted.

Chapter 14

Advertise to Create Business Wealth

Now you understand how writing a letter informing, enlightening, exciting and stimulating your prospect creates a higher reward for you, use the same principles in any media you use to deliver your message to your prospect.

Write in an interesting, thought-provoking way; follow virtually the same structure. Don't think just because you are using a different way of reaching your prospect he/she is going to behave or think differently.

How To Make Your Adverts Sell

As I said, many of the principles for writing a direct response marketing letter also apply to adverts.

Of course your advert does not run to multiple numbers of pages like your letters, unless you have a small fortune to spend.

It's important to start small with your advertising (e.g. with classifieds, as mentioned in *How to Guarantee Your Results* on page 109) and increase the size as the response covers the cost or creates a profit.

Never spend more than you can afford to lose if no-one takes up your offer.

There are two types of adverts, those used to raise

awareness – 'show adverts' – and those designed to get a direct response. I strongly advise you to concentrate on the latter, which should cover the cost - and more.

'Show' adverts are an expensive way of creating brand awareness large corporate organisations spend £millions on. There is absolutely no way of knowing how many people have even looked at the advert, let alone been inspired to do anything. (Actually I suspect very few sales are made as a direct result of these types of adverts).

So what's the difference?

Direct Response Adverts, as with direct response letters, are specifically created to stimulate the reader to **TAKE ACTION.**

The action could be to pick up the phone, complete and return an enquiry or order coupon, or take a voucher to a specific store.

The other thing you find on all successful *direct response adverts* is a code, which is used to monitor response (see *How to Guarantee Your Results* on page 109).

The by-product you gain from all of this marketing methodology is you automatically create 'brand awareness' as people buy from you.

Newsflash: People don't buy Newspapers or Magazines just to Read the Adverts!

People buy and read newspapers and magazines because they want to be informed or because they are interested in the news or articles they contain.

I'd guess the only person who buys a publication just to check the adverts, is the one who has placed an advert in it!

Adverts are an interruption. It is your job to attract the reader, create the interruption and distract him from the articles and news he is browsing.

The headline is even more important in your advertisement because it is jostling with all the other headlines, on articles and other advertisements.

Use a genuine and compelling headline. Include something specific about your offer or guarantee. Don't use a headline designed to catch attention if it doesn't have anything to do with your offer. Your reader feels cheated and he/she certainly does not read the whole advert and definitely does not respond to it.

The design and layout of your advert is critical. Large amounts of white space with cryptic or 'clever' slogans may be admired for being 'creative' or 'aesthetic' but won't get the sales your business needs.

Design your advert in the same way as your letter; it is still a '**Salesperson in Print**.'

This Single Technique Makes Your Advert Out-Perform Your Competitors

- Write your advertisement as if it is an article in the publication. And copy, as far as possible, the style of the publication you are placing your advert in.
- Organise your text into columns - the same as the publication you are running the advert in.
- Use 'Editorial' style in the main body copy with sub-headlines to draw the reader into specific sections of your advert.

(These adverts are sometimes referred to as 'advertorials'. The advantage for you is, you know what you write will appear, whereas if, for example, you sent a press release to the Editor it may not be published. And if it is, the printed article may not be what you had hoped for).

Why use an editorial style?

People take more notice of articles and editorials than they do of obvious adverts. The reader is inclined to believe and trust the content – whereas in an advertisement there is a predisposition to think – ***"Well they would say that wouldn't they?"***

Remember, it is your job to educate and inform the reader about the results your product or service provides and clearly describe why what you are offering is better than your competitors and how it benefits him/her.

- Describe the real benefits clearly in your advert.
- Keep your company logo as small as possible; perhaps even omit it altogether.

The reason for this is, unless you are a multi-national organisation with a well known brand name, the readers have not necessarily heard of you and therefore do not associate any specific benefits or image with your logo. Never plaster your logo all across the top of the advert - that's where your headline needs to be calling from.

- Use a response coupon in your advertisement. This is the equivalent of the request form in your direct mail letter.
- Use a reference or code on the coupon so you know which advert placed in which publication has generated the greatest response. (See *Monitor Your Responses* on page 112).
- Keep accurate records so you know what is – and what isn't - working.
- If there isn't room for a coupon, ask your callers to quote a reference code or include a code in your response address.

Include These 9 Elements to Make Your Advert Perform

As with a sales letter, there are certain elements to include, wherever possible, in your advert:

1. Headline – spend the majority of your time on this. It is the ATTENTION part of the AIDA acronym described earlier.

2. Promise - follow up on your promise in the headline. If you promised some key information in your main headline, tell them what it is. Keep your reader's INTEREST.

3. Offer - Describe exactly what you are offering, what it does for him, how he benefits. Keep in mind people do not like being 'sold to' - start to create his DESIRE.

4. Sub-headlines - use sub-headlines to draw the reader's eye to different parts of your advert.

5. Testimonial – people respond to other people's experiences and recommendations; even in advertisements. Include a testimonial or recommendation for your product or service. It can be from a satisfied customer or from a recognised expert in the field.

6. Lose – It is your job to make sure your reader cannot possibly ignore your offer. Make absolutely sure he understands exactly what he loses out on if he does not respond. Appeal to his emotional wants or desires. Make sure you supply enough detail to help him justify buying from you.

7. Repeat the benefits – raise the desire again to own or experience what you offer. Get your reader excited about responding to your advert. Add a bonus for responding.

8. Test Pictures - test your advert with and without a picture. Make sure the picture is appropriate and add a benefit focused caption underneath.

And then...

9. Action – tell him *exactly* what to do now; tell him to fill in the coupon and post it to the Freepost address.

Tell him to call the Freephone number and place their request NOW.

Or tell him to send an email confirming his interest.

Make it as easy as possible for your reader to follow through.

AIDA Gets it Right...

If you are placing a fairly small advert, and do not have room for *all* the elements I've described, follow the **AIDA** formula, as a minimum:

ATTENTION	–	headline to attract attention
INTEREST	–	create interest in your offer
DESIRE	–	stimulate the reader's desire for the real benefits and guarantees you are giving
ACTION	–	include a coded response coupon or mechanism he can use immediately.

With your smaller adverts use shorter, almost 'telegram' style sentences, to get the message across succinctly.

"A Picture Paints a Thousand Words – *or does it*?"

Graphics can draw the reader's eye to your advert. But, make sure whatever you use is interesting *and relevant.*

If the picture is not relevant it does not do your advert any favours. Be careful not to 'dupe' your audience into reading your advert. Doing so could create a subliminal barrier to reading any future adverts you place. For example; a scantily clad lady may attract a reader's attention, but is it really appropriate to your offer?

A curiosity picture, such as one showing the result of using your product, is more effective than a picture of the product itself.

Or use a photograph demonstrating the product being used 'in situ'. This encourages the reader to 'see' him or herself using it in the same situation.

Photographs normally gain a higher response than artwork. Your test will show what works best for you.

If you can show a photo of a personality or professional expert, using or endorsing your service or product, it lends more credibility to your advert.

Always add an informative caption to your picture. State the benefit of buying your product or service in the caption ...

"A benefit oriented caption underneath every picture you use can create a substantial increase in response to your advert"

Tests have shown people read the caption under a picture and, written in the right way; it can entice them to read the whole advert. Regard it as the equivalent of the

P.S. in your letter, which draws your reader in.

Use Your Advertising to Create Other Successes

If you are planning a large mailing campaign you may find testing your headlines in the classified ads helps you to find which headline gets the best response more quickly. You can then use the 2 pulling the highest result in a further test to part of your contact list.

This can be a comparatively inexpensive way of finding the best headlines to test with your target contact list in a direct mail campaign.

Chapter 15

Weave Your Web Page to Capture Your Prospect

How many times have you heard someone say "Oh, we've got a website. It looks very nice but we don't get any enquiries or sales from it."

If you go and look at the website I bet you it is the standard 'all about us' style, starting off with the 'Welcome' page.

This just doesn't work. It contains nothing of interest to the person browsing the web.

In fact, you have even less time to capture your visitor's attention on your website than you do with a letter or advert.

Think about it - *do you browse the web*? If you do, how often are you looking for information? Doing some research perhaps?

It's what the majority of people go onto the web to do.

This is why the standard 'corporate style brochure' on a web page really doesn't work.

Your website needs to capture your visitor, entice her to stay and browse further.

You can do this very easily; create a web site full of information. Full of useful 'nuggets' the visitor gets an immediate benefit from.

Or develop a site explaining, in mouth-watering detail, how a certain product or service creates the results they are looking for... and you are able to supply it. Now you are onto a winner.

People often bookmark a useful site like this and come back time and time again. And, at some stage, they buy from you.

Check these two examples:

http://www.your-diabetes.com
http://www.delvaux-acticoa.com

Direct Response Web Site Gathers Impressive Results

The most successful commercial website style is one that looks like a letter. The same style of letter you would write to your prospect following the principles in this book.

In fact, as with your letter, aim to promote a single product or service and gently, but inexorably, lead your visitor through to a specific action.

The action could be to subscribe to your e-newsletter. Or to download a free report or article - which gives them even more information about something very relevant to what you offer.

This type of website does not have numerous links and buttons at the top of the page, which could distract your visitor and entice them away from the important message in your web-letter.

What it does have is links to request the report or whatever else is being offered. These links, scattered throughout the letter, lead to a form for the visitor to complete so you capture, as a minimum, their first name and email address with permission to keep in touch.

Getting this permission is absolutely necessary if your visitor is located in a country with any sort of 'data protection' or privacy policy, as we have in the UK.

You can see an example of this direct-response, letter style at www.accelerateyoursales.co.uk where there is an offer to subscribe to a series of free reports. The reports are distilled versions of a few of the chapters in this book.

Reassure Your Visitor Constantly

At any point in the process of responding to your offer your visitor could change her mind and 'abandon' your site.

Write a good initial landing page on your website to gently persuade and convince her what you offer is of real benefit to her. Keep this supportive style throughout the request process.

Visit www.CarolBentley.com and subscribe to the free reports or take up the other offers so you can see for yourself the steps you are guided through.

When you click the link for the free reports you are taken to a response form. The form reaffirms your decision and the benefits you gain as a result. At the bottom of the form is a privacy statement - again to reassure you, the visitor, your details are not going to be misused. (Use code BKT01 to try it out).

Once the form is submitted a confirmation page appears. It congratulates you on making your decision and tells you, you are just a few moments away from discovering how to boost your sales results. It tells you to look out for the email containing your first report.

A friendly email is sent out asking you to confirm your request for the reports. This is to prevent you receiving something you didn't ask for (and so I don't get accused of spamming!) – in case someone else has used your email address. Once you confirm your subscription you receive your first report with a message thanking you for subscribing.

Discover Your Target Market Through Your Website

Use a direct response website offering a free report to find your target audience. People who are interested in what you describe 'hold up their hand' by requesting the report.

Design your website to ask for your visitor's email address, as a minimum, so she can receive the download link for the report. You have now captured her information, which you can add to your database.

Now you have her details you can nurture the relationship with informative emails until she is happy to purchase from you.

This is an inexpensive way to acquire your targeted contact list.

It's important to remember the World Wide Web is not a magical source of wealth and information; it doesn't just 'appear'. You have to do some work yourself. For example, if you are researching you would normally use the search engines, such as Google or Yahoo, to find the information you want.

If you are looking for visitors, or sales on a commercial site, you have to *drive* people to your site. You can do this through advertising (e.g. classified adverts), in your letters, brochures and when you are talking to people.

And, of course, submitting your site to the search engines and using a wide variety of internet marketing activities and tools.

Creating a flow of visitors to your website is a specialist subject which is not covered in this book but, if you want to discover examples of different internet marketing techniques, check out Ed Rivis' 'Online Marketing Tactics For SME Success' blog website at http://www.EdRivis.com

Want to Know How to Create Your Own Results Generating Website?

Without paying a fortune for little or no results?

Anyone can succeed on the Net with the right words and the right process.

Having read this book you know how to create compelling sales letters. For your website you just need to adjust and fine-tune this same skill.

And it all starts with the same core business-building foundation...

"Information..."

People on the Net are looking for information... *Quality content.* Quality content is what builds traffic and delivers sales to your business. In other words, **write better... to sell more!**

I discovered **The Netwriting Masters Course** shows you how to "write for success" and build a profitable, stable, online business. It's very do-able... you just need to bring your own brain power and motivation!

So why am I giving away this valuable course for free?

It's a simple answer... **I want you to succeed.**

I've given you the insider knowledge to create a more effective marketing process for your business offline. And in this chapter 15 I emphasise, on the web, 'Content is king' as well.

Your <u>FREE</u> 50-page Netwriting Masters Course...

Builds on your new writing skills to help you create your own results generating website.

The Internet has incredible business building opportunities waiting to be grabbed!

Take advantage of its powerful potential. The **Netwriting Masters Course** provides the 2-step process to harness that potential for your business and produce results... traffic and sales...

Send an email to:

webwriting@aweber.com

To get your **FREE** 50-page PDF Netwriting Masters course **today**.

Chapter 16

Enhance Your Company Image with Newsletters

Follow the same informative style for anything you use to make contact with your customer or prospect. This applies equally to newsletters.

People crave knowledge and understanding. Keeping people informed in a way they find useful and interesting encourages them to do business with you.

9 Mistakes People Make in Newsletters

Newsletters are an ideal way of keeping your customers, and prospects, up to date with information about your products or services and anything happening in your company.

You can make your newsletter effective by making sure you don't make these mistakes:

Mistake 1.   Boring Headlines

Use descriptive headlines, same as in a letter, to attract your reader's interest. Give the promise of something worth reading. You can turn a boring headline into something more appealing by simply expanding it as in the examples below:

Boring Headline: New XL987 Widget

Interesting Headline: New XL987 Widget
Increases Production by 30%

Boring Headline: New Website Launched
Interesting Headline: Download Free Report
from Newly Launched Website

Boring Headline: Message from the Managing
Director
Interesting Headline: Managing Director
Announces New Process Cuts Delivery Times
in Half

Use the 'Attention' Words on page 55 to give your
Newsletter headline more impact.

Mistake 2. Headlines Are The Same Size

Glance through any newspaper and you see the
headlines are different sizes. It makes the paper
more attractive to look at and guides the reader to
more important articles.

Design your newsletter to do the same. Generate
more interest in your main stories with larger
headlines and use smaller headlines in those that are
less significant.

Mistake 3. Woolly Opening Sentences.

Keep your reader's attention with your opening
sentence.

Once your reader has been caught by the headline,
don't disappoint her with a boring statement; it
discourages her from finishing the article.

For example if you are writing the article in an in-
house company newsletter for the XL987 widget
headline an uninteresting start might be:

The new XL987 widget was launched at the company AGM on July 18th in London.

Your reader doesn't care when or where the new product was launched - the sentence offers nothing of real interest to her at all. Whereas this one clearly states something more remarkable:

"As well as increasing production by 30%, the new XL987 widget will cut costs by 10% and is likely to add £147,000 to the company turnover," claimed Managing Director, Charles Forthwith, at the AGM.

Newspaper reporters know they must get the most important information over first. You must do the same.

Mistake 4. Too Many Font Styles

Resist the temptation to 'pretty up' your newsletter with a myriad of font styles and colours. It makes your newsletter too busy and difficult for people to read. It also looks very amateurish.

Choose a maximum of 2 fonts - 1 for headlines and 1 for the main body of the text. You can change the size of the headline font to create variety - as previously mentioned.

Do not change the font size for the articles. Write enough text to fill the space you have. Don't increase the size to fit a gap or reduce the size to fit more in. It looks inconsistent and unattractive.

Mistake 5. Using a Sans Serif Font in the Body Text

Make your articles easy to read. Serif fonts (with the small tail on the letters) are easier on the eyes.

Always use a serif font for the main body of the newsletter's text. (See *Plain is Best...* on page 81).

If your reader finds it a strain to read the text they abandon your newsletter and certainly won't look out for your next issue.

Mistake 6. Using Single Column Layout

Emulate a newspaper and split your text into columns.

Vary the number of columns your article is spread across and use a highlight colour to make articles stand out. (A highlight colour is a background tint behind the text. It breaks up the page and lessens a 'flat' appearance).

Split your articles over pages (again as newspapers do) to encourage your reader to turn the page.

Mistake 7. Not Allowing Sufficient Time

Creating a newsletter requires a heavy time commitment. If you do not fully anticipate the amount of time it takes there's a good chance it all becomes 'just too much' and falls by the wayside.

This could be damaging to your professional image and credibility.

If you are not used to researching and writing articles you can expect to take up to 7 hours to produce enough material, proof-read and edited, for each single A4 side. If you design and develop the layout ready for printing as well, you need to add even more time.

You may decide it is worth getting a professional newsletter writer and producer to do the work for you.

Chapter 17

How to Create Brochures and Catalogues

Brochures and catalogues should not be treated any differently to your letters, web pages and newsletters. They are still a method of communicating with your customer or prospect, who still wants information.

Mistakes Most Company Brochures Make

Nearly every company brochure I see starts off with a large logo, the company name and maybe the address as well.

It explains at great length how professional the company is, how focused <u>they are</u> on customer care or their quality control or their wonderful production processes.

The brochure rarely expands on any of these 'facts' to explain how this benefits the reader and, I suspect, the vast majority of them do very little for the company's sales result.

A brochure written in a descriptive style, focused on the real result the reader gains, extolling how all the company's experience gives the reader an incredibly wonderful outcome, always performs considerably better than the competitor's 'corporate' style brochure.

If your brochure (or catalogue) is promoting products you sell, use the text to describe how the item can be used and the result or benefit the user enjoys. Do not give just a simple, brief product specification - as most catalogues do.

Use photographs of people using or wearing your product (as appropriate). Tests have shown photographs showing a product in use or the effect it bestows always out-pulls items in a static photo.

Request for Professional Services

Carol,

Copywriting is a skill that definitely boosts sales and can help my <u>business to grow</u> and I'd like some professional help.

Please send information about these products/services:

❑   'I Want to Buy Your Product..' Audio and Workbook

❑   The Complete Home-Study for Writing Stunning, Responsive Sales Letters (Recording of Live Workshop)

❑   Copywriting Teleconference Course

❑   Live, Copywriting Workshops

❑   Expert Review of my Sales Copy

❑   Marketing Mentoring with Expert Copywriting Services

❑   Professional Copywriting Services

Please Use Block Capitals

Mr/Mrs/Miss/Ms _____ Name _____

Address_____

_____

_____ Postcode_____

Telephone No _____

Please send important information on new releases by email to:

_____

Visit: **www.carolbentley.com** for free reports & valuable information.

Post your request to:
PYB Ltd, FREEPOST NATW661, Swanage, BH19 1BR

Chapter 18

Preparing to Write

Have you ever been preparing for a party or an evening out and suddenly discovered you haven't got everything you need? It's disrupting isn't it? If it is an important evening or event it can even be stressful.

This is why many people plan ahead; listing everything they need when organising an event, so nothing is missed.

Preparing to write your sales letter is the same. If you don't have that 'all important' information to hand, you have to interrupt and break your flow of concentration to find what you need. What's more you'll probably find it much more difficult to get going again.

Have Everything to Hand to Make Writing Easier...

Take the time to gather everything together you are going to need whilst you are writing your letter.

Consider these (they are repeated in the *Writer's Preparation Checklist*):

- **What is your business (product / service)?**

Write a brief statement describing your product or service. E.g. *Multi-Size Battery Charger complete with rechargeable batteries.* Or *Computer Training Services*

Expand your description a bit further:

• If you are offering a product what does it do? How does it work? How is it used?

The Battery Charger will recharge two popular sizes of battery, AA, and AAA. It can be used with the mains electric or in a car using the cigarette-lighter adaptor supplied. Each battery has its own charge level indicator so you can see how much power each contains and the progress of the charging. When the batteries are in place the clear cover can be closed to keep them secure. This is particularly useful when transporting the charger and batteries together.

• If you are offering a service: What is it? Consultancy? Training? Legal or Accounting services?

The Computer Training is customised to the business needs. An evaluation is carried out beforehand of the delegates existing skills. The company requirements are identified and a training programme is developed to bring the individual's skill-set up to the level required by the company.

• What is the normal price?

• What is the lifetime value of an average customer? What can you afford to invest when finding new business? (See *Know What Your Customer is Worth* on page 13).

• What is your offer in this letter? Is there a special introductory saving? Limited-time offer? 2-for-1 sale? Free information? Why are you making this offer?

Giving 'reasons why' creates credibility in your prospect's mind. It could be you want to demonstrate your product or service or maybe you have an overstock and are offering items at half-price or less.

• **What are the features of your product or service?**
Make a note of all the facts and specifications.
E.g. *Battery Charger Package Contains:*

Fast charger.
Mains power adapter (UK plug for 220 - 240V operation)
Car lighter adapter lead.
USB connection lead.
4 x 2400mAh high quality NiMH batteries.

Technical Specifications:
-dV & 0dV control.
Over-temperature sensing.
Charge times: (Approximate)
2 x 2400mAh AA: 2.5 hours
4 x 2400mAh AA: 5 hours
2 x 700mAh AAA: 1 hour

Note: This charger can charge 2 or 4 AA size batteries, but only 2 AAA batteries at a time.

• **What are the main benefits it offers? What does it do for** your prospect? What specific problem does it solve? How does it make or save money? Save time or work? Make life easier or better? Remember, your reader is thinking *"What's In It for Me?"*

Battery Charger:

Saves money – especially if you need a lot of batteries or are using equipment that is power-hungry and drains batteries quickly.

With this unit you can see the exact state of the batteries. You don't have to watch for the 'green' light indicator or, as with some chargers, monitor the time the batteries have been charging where the only indicator is a red charging light.

Computer Training:

We only cover subjects that are needed so time is not wasted. Plus on a standard course you will often find 40% of the subject matter is not relevant or delegates already know it, whereas these are focused training sessions. The company gets the skills they need and attendees are motivated because it is directly linked to the work they are doing.

• **What are the secondary benefits?** Secondary benefits may be as relevant to your prospect as your (perceived) main benefits. In some cases where there is more than one strong benefit and result it is worth sending a letter describing one benefit and another describing the second benefit to see which creates the strongest appeal.

• **What information, service or result does it give that your prospect cannot get anywhere else?** Or how and why is it new, better than, different from what's already available? Is it unique or exclusive? Why is it better than the competition?

• **What is the purpose of writing?** Do you want people to ask for information? Buy something? Send for something FREE? Visit your premises? Visit your stand at a trade show or exhibition?

• **What's your budget?** Remember to include production costs such as graphic design work, printing, paper, envelopes, posting, telephone-follow up etc. Also allow time and money for testing.

• When is it to be completed? Is there a publishing deadline? Or an event date or time-limitation in the offer? Have you allowed enough time to prepare your letter ready to go out to your list?

• Who is your main prospect? In business; what's his or her title and responsibility? What are his/her biggest concerns, fears, attitudes, possible objections? How can he/she use your product to get ahead or keep up?

Create the Right Environment to Write

Now you've got everything together you can start preparing <u>yourself</u>.

First of all make sure your environment is conducive to writing. Can you write with background noise going on? Or does it distract you? If you suddenly hear something does it drag your attention away from your writing? If this happens to you, you need to find somewhere quiet where you won't be disturbed.

Now are you comfortable in yourself? It may sound silly, but I find it very difficult to write when I'm feeling hungry. It's as if my stomach starts protesting and until it is satisfied it is just not going to let me get on with anything creative!

Are you too warm or too cool? If you are too warm you may get drowsy and then you certainly won't get your letter written. Too cool and you may find your fingers become difficult to move - whether hand-writing or typing.

Is the ambience of the room you are using right? Does it create the right mood for you to work in and develop the letter for your offer? If the room is 'cluttered' does it prevent you thinking 'clearly'?

Very often 'writer's block' can be attributed to your

surroundings and environment.

Handling Writer's Block

There are all sorts of reasons for what we call 'writer's block'. Sometimes it's as simple as not knowing how to get started when faced with a blank screen or piece of paper.

This is where the 'outline' can help, acting as a catalyst to your thoughts and ideas. (See *Outline of a Successful Letter* on page 77

Different people get over writer's block in different ways. Here are a few suggestions you might find works for you:

How to 'kick-start' your writing

Start off with **"I am writing about..."** and continue the sentence. Just keep writing. At this stage it doesn't matter what you write.

It's a bit like trying to 'jump-start' a car. It doesn't matter if the initial part of the journey is slow - and probably jerky - once the engine catches it smoothes out.

Your writing may start off a 'little jerky'; disjointed even, but eventually your thoughts 'drop into gear' and you are on a roll.

It's always easier to write about something you feel passionate about - and because you feel passionate about your business you soon find you slip into the 'higher gears' and the words flow from your fingertips.

Relax into a writing mood

There are some days when even this simple kick-start is not going to work. Many professional writers get themselves into the right state or 'frame of mind' for writing by visualising:

First of all look over your 'Writer's Preparation Checklist'. (See '*27 Questions to Prepare You for Writing*' on page 151).

Now, relax in your chair, take some deep, slow breaths.

Visualise your muscles relaxing from your toes, up through your ankles, legs, body, chest, arms and fingers.

Imagine the stress and tension dripping out of your fingers.

Now, close your eyes and think about the last time you were enjoying writing freely. It may have been when you were writing to a friend or relative. Or maybe even your lover.

Create a picture in your mind of yourself as if you are doing it now.

Notice how you are sitting; your environment.

What are you feeling as you write? Is it excitement? Are you calm and in control? Or are you just enjoying putting your feelings and thoughts onto paper?

What are you thinking? Are there lots of different thoughts running around in your head? Or are your thoughts quite ordered and structured?

What's the expression on your face? Are you concentrating? Smiling? Or just relaxed and calm?

Are there any sounds? If so, notice what they are and where they are coming from. Are they behind you? To your left, right or in front? Maybe they are inside your head? Again, just be aware of them.

By doing this you are re-creating the state you were in when you were writing easily, without any tension or pressure. You were enjoying the experience and *that* is what you want to do whilst writing your sales letter.

When you have immersed yourself fully in the experience, think about what you want to write about today.

What is the purpose for writing? Do you want your sales letter to create enquiries? Or do you want people to place an order? Or do you want them to visit your website or attend a function?

Think of a statement which clearly defines what you want to achieve with this letter.

Now, open your eyes, write down the statement you've just thought of and start your first sentence: "This is about..." and continue.

Energise your writing creativity

Still having problems? Exercise energises you, frees your mind and allows your creativity to come to the fore.

Go for a walk, jogging or running. Perhaps you like horse-riding, whatever physical activity you enjoy helps to 'free' your mind.

In fact, just getting away from your normal environment, away from the phones and other people helps.

Even stepping outside your normal four walls can be therapeutic. You suddenly find you are flooded with ideas and your writing begins to flow when you return to your writing area.

When you go out for exercise, take a small notepad and pen or a portable recorder with you. Whilst you are getting some fresh air and exercise ideas and thoughts often just 'pop in' to your head. You must capture these.

If you try to remember these little gems, rather than writing them down, the really good ones disappear.

Think about it... if you've just said something in a conversation and someone asks you to repeat *exactly* what you said, there is a very good chance you won't be able to remember the precise words you used.

The same happens if you try to 'remember' that perfect headline or phrase you've just thought of, which explains precisely what you mean. Unless, of course, you are blessed with a photographic memory.

Use others to inspire you

Read other good sales letters. They don't have to be from your company or even the same profession or industry. When you find a sales letter that enthrals and fascinates you, explore the possibility of adapting the style to your offer. Do be careful though, don't use the same words or you could fall foul of the copyright laws.

There are many ways you can overcome writer's block. Everyone is different and you will discover some tactics work for you - and others don't. Once you know what works best for you, you'll be more relaxed and can start your writing.

Your Practical Checklists – Copy and Use

Chapter 19

Your Practical Checklists - Copy and Use

Checklist: 27 Questions to Prepare You for Writing

Use this checklist to make sure you have gathered everything you need to make writing your sales letter as easy and effortless as possible.

1. **What is your business (product / service)?** Write a brief statement describing your product or service.

2. **If you are offering a product** what does it do? How does it work? How is it used?

3. **If you are offering a service:** What is it? Consultancy? Training? Legal or Accounting services?

4. **What is the normal price?**

5. **What is the lifetime value of your average customer?** How much you can afford to spend on finding new customers. (See *Know What Your Customer is Worth* on page 13).

6. **What is your offer in this letter?** Is there a special introductory saving? Limited-time offer? 2-for-1 sale? Free information? Why are you making this offer?

7. **What are the features of your product or service?** All facts and specifications.

8. **What are the main benefits it offers?** What does it do for your prospect?

9. **What are the secondary benefits?**

10. **What information, service or result does it give that your prospect cannot get anywhere else?** Or how and why is it new, better than, different from what's already available?

11. **What is the purpose of writing?** What action do you want people to take?

12. **What's your overall campaign budget?**

13. **When is it to be completed?**

14. **Who is your main prospect?**

15. **Do you have your secondary prospects? Who are they?**

16. **Where will you get your prospects from?**

17. **Can you make your offer tangible?** Do you have

a sample?

18. **Do you have copies of previous sales letters?**

19. **Have you got all your testimonials and endorsements to hand?**

20. **Do you have any information about any complaints your company has received and how they were handled?**

21. **Which tests are you planning to use?** Different headlines, price, offer, result and benefit?

22. **What must you include in your letter**, e.g. specific limitations of use.

23. **What must never be said or promised?**

24. **Compared against your competitors why are you better?**

25. **How do you want people to pay if you are asking for an order?**

26. **How do you want people to respond?**

27. **What guarantee are you offering?**

Checklist: 20 Points to Make Your Sales Letter Compelling

Use this check list to help you make sure you are writing your letter in the most effective way to gain the highest response possible.

1. Your letter is written to satisfy one or more of the appeals listed on page 53.

   ❑ Yes ❑ No

2. Your headline uses compelling, 'attention' words (See *79 'Attention' words & phrases to draw your readers in...* on page 55.

   ❑ Yes ❑ No

3. Your headline or opening sentence is strong, specific and results orientated. (See *Your Headline Can Make or Break Your Results...* on page 51).

   ❑ Yes ❑ No

4. In a letter, you have a good, compelling P.S.

   ❑ Yes ❑ No

5. Your letter uses these evocative words wherever possible:

You	Free
Money	Save
Guarantee	Easy
Love	New
Results	Health
Proven	Discovery
Safety	New

   ❑ Yes ❑ No

6. Your letter uses the different base languages to create

the greatest rapport with your reader (See *Use the Right Language to Cut Through Communication Barriers* on page 18).

❑ Yes ❑ No

7. You are not over-using the words: 'We', 'My' 'Us' or 'Our(s)'.

❑ Yes ❑ No

8. Your sales message is emotional not analytical or logical. It 'paints the picture' (See *Make Your Offer Compelling* on page 65).

❑ Yes ❑ No

9. You are not talking about you or your company rather than the offer you are making.

❑ Yes ❑ No

10. Your letter highlights the results your prospect enjoys when they he/she has your product or service – not just the features.

❑ Yes ❑ No

11. The content of your letter is informative, not 'clever' or 'amusing'.

❑ Yes ❑ No

12. You are making an offer in your letter your prospect can respond to.

❑ Yes ❑ No

13. Your offer is the best you can make.

❑ Yes ❑ No

14. You are not giving your prospect too many choices – only sell '1 thing at a time'.

❑ Yes ❑ No

15. You are including a guarantee to remove the risk of buying from your prospect. (See *A Guarantee Makes it Easy for Your Prospect to Buy...* on page 71).
❑ Yes ❑ No

16. You have included testimonials from your satisfied customers / clients or a recognised expert.
❑ Yes ❑ No

17. Your response form and instructions are easy to use and follow. (See *Design a Responsive Order Form* on page 89).
❑ Yes ❑ No

18. You have an effective system to measure responses and where they have come from. (See *How to Guarantee Your Results* on page 109).
❑ Yes ❑ No

19. You are able to fulfil any response you receive to your offer.
❑ Yes ❑ No

20. If the letter is highly successful you are ready to send it out to more new prospects immediately.
❑ Yes ❑ No

Checklist: 31 Points for Your Order Form Design

Compare your response form against this checklist to make sure you haven't forgotten anything important. Checking also makes sure your form is easy to use and not a barrier to your prospect responding.

1.   Does Your Form Have a Descriptive Name such as Priority Reservation, Special Enquiry or Delegate Certificate?

     ❑ Yes   ❑ No

2.   Is your order form on a separate sheet of paper?

     ❑ Yes   ❑ No

3.   Is the back of the form blank?

     ❑ Yes   ❑ No

4.   Does your form have a border?

     ❑ Yes   ❑ No

5.   Is your form printed on heavy quality paper?

     ❑ Yes   ❑ No

6.   Is the paper used for your form OK for all pen types?

     ❑ Yes   ❑ No

7.   Have you started with tick boxes and 'Yes' at the beginning of the form?

     ❑ Yes   ❑ No

8.   Does your form re-state the benefits and results of your offer in positive statements?

     ❑ Yes   ❑ No

9.   Is your guarantee repeated in a shaded or boxed panel?

     ❑ Yes   ❑ No

10. Does the form show the cut-off time (if there is one)?
    ❑ Yes   ❑ No

11. Is the form simple to fill in?
    ❑ Yes   ❑ No

12. Have you asked for the form to be completed in Block Capitals?
    ❑ Yes   ❑ No

13. Have you allowed room for a quantity to be added (if appropriate)?
    ❑ Yes   ❑ No

14. Is your wording crystal clear?
    ❑ Yes   ❑ No

15. Have you included space for full contact details, including email addresses?
    ❑ Yes   ❑ No

16. Have you started the contact details with Mr/Mrs/Miss/Ms?
    ❑ Yes   ❑ No

17. Have you given enough lines for long addresses?
    ❑ Yes   ❑ No

18. Have you shown a separate line for the postcode?
    ❑ Yes   ❑ No

19. Have you asked for permission to use your responder's email address?
    ❑ Yes   ❑ No

20. Have you included an opt-out box for further offers or information?
    ❑ Yes   ❑ No

21. Is your postal address on the order form?
    ❑ Yes   ❑ No

22. Have you included an opt-out box for offers or information from other organisations?

        ❏ Yes   ❏ No

23. Is your response form coded for monitoring responses?

        ❏ Yes   ❏ No

24. If payment is by cheque, have you said who to make the cheque payable to?

        ❏ Yes   ❏ No

25. If payment can be made by credit card or switch, have you given enough room for the card numbers, expiry dates, issue date (switch), security code and signature?

        ❏ Yes   ❏ No

26. Have you told the customer what to do with the completed form?

        ❏ Yes   ❏ No

27. If you are using a fax-back form, have you kept shading and heavy graphics to a minimum?

        ❏ Yes   ❏ No

28. If you are using a fax-back form, have you checked the size is OK for a fax machine?

        ❏ Yes   ❏ No

29. Have you asked your purchaser to refer a friend or colleague?

        ❏ Yes   ❏ No

30. Have you included a 'Thank You' note?

        ❏ Yes   ❏ No

31. Have you asked someone else to test the simplicity of the form by filling it out?

        ❏ Yes   ❏ No

What Are Your Results?

Dear Reader,

The powerful techniques, described in this book, have produced outstanding results for the companies that have used them.

I would love to learn about the successes <u>you</u> have gained by following these principles.

Please write and tell me about your experiences. What did you do differently and what impact did that have for you and your business? How has using this methodology improved your results?

You may write to me or you can send an email to: success@CarolBentley.com

Carol Bentley
c/o Promote Your Business
104 Victoria Avenue
Swanage
Dorset
BH19 1AS

I look forward to hearing about your triumphs.

Kind regards,

Carol A E Bentley
Author

Priority Request Form

❑   The information contained in this book has proved so effective I want to order additional copies for my friends and colleagues.

I also understand I can claim a quantity discount as shown in the table below:

Quantity Discount		Discounted Price Each	Qty Required	Total £
1 copy		£14.97		
2-4 copies	10%	£13.47		
5-9 copies	15%	£12.73		
10-19 copies	20%	£11.98		
20-49 copies	25%	£11.23		
50-99 copies	30%	£10.48		
100+ copies	50%	£7.49		
			Total:	
Free p&p to any full UK postal address				

I am enclosing a cheque for £ _____ made payable to Promote Your Business Ltd.

Mr/Mrs/Miss/Ms:		Name:		Surname:	
Position:					
Company:					
Address:					
Postcode:					
Telephone:					
Email Address*:					

* Please supply your email address ONLY if you want to receive information about future offers.

Send the completed form (photocopies are acceptable if you don't want to tear this page out) to:
PYB Ltd, 104 Victoria Avenue, Swanage, BH19 1AS, UK

"How to Banish Forever the Hair-Tearing Frustrations of Microsoft® Word® When Writing Your Sales Letters"

Dear Reader

You're busy typing up your letter, concentrating on making it as compelling as possible. And Microsoft® Word® decides to 'help' you and asks "Are you writing a letter?"

Of course you're writing a *@*# letter – and you don't need the program's interference.

You want to leave a single line of the paragraph at the end of this page or maybe push the last line of the paragraph onto the next page. Word won't let you. Grrr!

You want to use bullet points or numbered paragraphs with a nice line space between, but whenever you try to leave a line gap Word cancels your bullets or numbers. *"For pities sake – why can't you leave me alone"* you moan.

You want to split words at the end of the line so your reader's eye is drawn on to the next line but Word doesn't like splitting words – tough on you!

You want to indent the first line on every paragraph – why do you have to press the tab key **every** time you start a new paragraph? Can't Word do it for you?

Trouble is the 'help' from Microsoft® Word is intensely irritating when you know <u>exactly</u> what you want to do – *and the program does something entirely different*!

The good news is...

FREE Report Offer

You <u>can</u> stop Microsoft® Word® 'taking over' your document with these 29, simple to implement, techniques.

You see, I'm one of those strange people who actually get on OK with Word – probably something to do with using it for writing mountains of material for so many years. ☺ And that's why I know **exactly** how to switch off all those irritating features that drive you to distraction every day.

Now you can discover how to tame Word so you can do what <u>you want to do</u> and <u>when you want to do it</u>.

To get your report please supply your name, company and address and email address. Your report will be sent, in PDF format, by email. (Please note we do not send reports to free email addresses such as Hotmail etc. Use your company or subscribed ISP email). Please add info@CarolBentley.com to your email whitelist/address book to make sure you are able to receive this report.

Choose how you want to send your details from one of the following:

1. Write to: Free Word Report
Promote Your Business Ltd
104 Victoria Avenue,
Swanage BH19 1AS, UK

2. Email to: word@CarolBentley.com

3. Call with your request: 0800 015 55 15

Printed in the United Kingdom
by Lightning Source UK Ltd.
131272UK00001B/79-258/A